The United States and the European Community in a Transformed World

CHATHAM HOUSE PAPERS

A European Programme Publication
Programme Director: Susie Symes

The Royal Institute of International Affairs, at Chatham House in London, has provided an impartial forum for discussion and debate on current international issues for some 70 years. Its resident research fellows, specialized information resources, and range of publications, conferences, and meetings span the fields of international politics, economics, and security. The Institute is independent of government.

Chatham House Papers are short monographs on current policy problems which have been commissioned by the RIIA. In preparing the papers, authors are advised by a study group of experts convened by the RIIA, and publication of a paper indicates that the Institute regards it as an authoritative contribution to the public debate. The Institute does not, however, hold opinions of its own; the views expressed in this publication are the responsibility of the authors.

CHATHAM HOUSE PAPERS

The United States and the European Community in a Transformed World

**Michael Smith and
Stephen Woolcock**

The Royal Institute of International Affairs

Pinter Publishers
London

© Royal Institute of International Affairs, 1993

First published in Great Britain in 1993 by
Pinter Publishers Limited
25 Floral Street, London WC2E 9DS

British Library Cataloguing in Publication Data

A CIP catalogue record for this book is available from the British Library

ISBN 0-86187-098-0 (Paperback)
     0-86187-097-2 (Hardback)

Reproduced from copy supplied by
Koinonia Limited
Printed and bound in Great Britain by
Biddles Ltd

CONTENTS

ACKNOWLEDGMENTS

This Chatham House Paper was prepared as part of the research activities of the European Programme of the Royal Institute of International Affairs, directed by Susie Symes. The authors gratefully acknowledge the support of the Ford Foundation, which funded the research on which this volume is based. Close cooperation and mutual support from the Council on Foreign Relations in New York, which has been running a parallel project also funded by the Ford Foundation, greatly enriched our own work. We thank all those associated with the project for their help, in particular Gregory Treverton, Michael Aho and Bruce Stokes.

This volume concludes a two-stage project on EC–US relations. The results of the first stage were presented in an earlier Chatham House Paper, Stephen Woolcock's *Market Access Issues in EC–US Relations: Trading Partners or Trading Blows?*, published in December 1991.

It is standard practice at the RIIA to hold study groups to discuss work in progress. A series of meetings was held in London, and we would like to thank all the participants from Europe and America who contributed. We also thank those people, on both sides of the Atlantic, who were prepared to meet with us and discuss EC–US relations.

Both authors would like to thank Professor Helen Wallace, under whose direction the project was initiated and carried out, for her advice and encouragement. We are grateful to Pauline Wickham and Hannah Doe for editorial work on the volume, and to Alex Bellinger for organizing study groups and conferences in London and Washington.

October 1992   Michael Smith and Stephen Woolcock

1

THE CHALLENGES OF A TRANSFORMED WORLD

Speaking to the Berlin Press Club in December 1989, in the immediate aftermath of the fall of the Berlin Wall, US Secretary of State James Baker called for the construction of a new 'Euro-Atlantic architecture' centred on the United States and the European Community. This initial call was followed during 1990 by successive appeals from US policymakers, and by the negotiation of a Transatlantic Declaration signed by the US government and the EC in November 1990. The Declaration established procedures for consultation and regular interaction between Washington and Brussels, and appeared to form a reliable basis for the development of a working partnership, within the context of a 'Euro-Atlantic community' – now seen as extending from Vancouver to Vladivostok and encompassing economic, political and security dimensions.[1]

Historically speaking, the Transatlantic Declaration falls recognizably into a pattern of evolving relations between the United States and its European partners. By establishing procedural conventions and stressing the mechanisms for the realization of assumed common interests, it encapsulates the notion that Atlantic partnership can be built on deep structures of shared needs in the political, economic and security fields. By creating a means for the more effective conduct of US/EC relations, as opposed to relations within NATO or between the United States and individual West European governments, it reflects the perception that the United States and the Community form one leg of a 'triangle' in which the coexisting alliance and national (bilateral) relationships will continue to form an essential feature. As such, it can be seen as the product of at least three, and more plausibly four, decades of interaction and learning between American and European institutions and policy elites.[2]

1

The changes of the early 1990s, however, raise fundamental questions about the adequacy of historical learning and the accumulated perceptions and institutions of European/American relations. It is therefore important to explore the nature of the changes which have occurred or are occurring, and to evaluate their potential impact on the relations between the USA and a uniting Europe. Our position is clearly stated: radical changes in the nature of European international relations and in their links to US policies have created a need for a redefinition of the US/EC relationship as a central element in global and regional systems. Such arguments reflect not only the specific development of 'Europe', but also important changes in the United States itself as well as in the global system generally. They raise key questions about the nature of any redefinition, about the respective roles of the United States and the EC in the process of redefinition, and about the ways in which these must be reassessed in the transformed situation of the 1990s. Our focus in this study will be on the issues of economic and political change, and on those aspects of security that fall within an economic and political context, rather than on 'hard' defence policy and alliance issues, which are well covered elsewhere in the literature.[3]

The assertion that much has changed does not mean that forty years of history, of accumulated experience, institutions and expectations, must be discarded. The evolution of US/EC relations has passed through a number of more or less well-defined phases, and each of these has laid down sediments of policy and practice. But the challenges of the 1990s cannot be met simply by the invocation of assumed shared interests, needs or expectations. We have evidence of this from a growing list of events and developments during the past years, many of them symbolizing real policy dilemmas and demands:

- During 1991 and 1992, the framework of US/EC economic relations continued to be shaken by the immediate problems of agreement in the Uruguay Round. But this was merely a symptom of more fundamental structural problems, such as the strengthening of the EC's economic muscle relative to that of the US and a continued growth in economic interdependence without commensurate progress in policy convergence between the two sides. These difficulties raise questions about the respective roles of the EC and the US in the world economy, and about how the two entities can cope with the linkages between domestic structures and the demands of ever more integrated economies.
- At the same time, the need to think through the changing role of

2

NATO in a transformed Europe, and to meet specific challenges to the international order ranging from the collapse of the USSR to the onset of civil war in Yugoslavia, brought home the importance of new political thinking in the Western alliance. As in the case of the economic framework, it has been apparent that questions of role and the interaction between American and Community concerns have been central to the ways in which the US and the EC have coped with the challenges.

– As well as being caught up in transformations in the global and regional systems, both the United States and the Community have been engaged in a process of self-examination and redefinition, creating tensions between internal and external priorities. This has been focused, in the United States, by the 1992 Presidential election campaign and, in the Community, by the processes surrounding the Maastricht agreements.

The nature and impact of transformation

If transformed circumstances demand a redefined Euro-Atlantic relationship, then our first task must be to explore the nature of the transformation itself. In the remainder of this chapter, a number of dimensions will be identified and their implications assessed. In particular, the following areas are examined:

(1) The evidence for radical structural change affecting European/American relations, and for the impact of new policy and issue linkages on the United States and the Community.
(2) The problem of policy consistency in conditions of complex interdependence and multidimensional linkages, particularly as it affects the definition and pursuit of common interests.
(3) The problems of burden-sharing in a transformed context, and of managing institutional diversity in the Atlantic and global arenas, whether this be through formal institutional processes or less formal conventions and 'rules of the game'.

The final part of the chapter addresses the requirements and conditioning factors of a redefined Euro-Atlantic relationship.

What is the evidence that Euro-Atlantic relations have experienced and are experiencing radical structural change in the 1990s? To our mind, three elements are central to the inquiry. In the first place, a substantial rebalancing in the world economy has occured, in which the changed positions of the United States and the Community are a key feature. Clearly, there are other elements in this shift, not least the position of Japan and newly industrializing economies, but the fact remains: the respective economic weights of the USA and the EC have changed, and this is recognized to have important policy, institutional and related effects. In particular, there is a kind of perceptual shift emerging, on the one hand, from a process of 'self-recognition' on the part of the Community and, on the other, from the increasing self-doubt of American policy and industrial elites. In the early stages of the EC's single market programme, this conjunction took its most explicit form in the suspicions about 'fortress Europe'; it was then underlined by the evidence of problems in the Uruguay Round. Interestingly, the potential implications of the Maastricht agreement on economic and monetary union did not create equivalent US concerns about the role of the Community in international monetary policy. This will be discussed in more detail in Chapter 3. In the current policy debate these structural changes are often linked to the question of regionalization – in the shape, first and foremost, of European economic integration, but also of moves towards the creation of a North American Free Trade Area (NAFTA).[4]

Second, the United States and the Community find themselves in a new global and European political context, fundamentally shaped by the collapse of Soviet rule and by the emergence of a fragile new system of states in central and eastern Europe and what used to be the Soviet Union. At present, this is a transformed context without a settled structure and without accepted institutional shape, either at the international or – in many instances – at the national level. Beyond Europe, there are persistent questions arising from the intersection of regional security complexes with the global balance of power and military weight. For the Community, the transformation has fed into and fed upon the process of increasing self-recognition in the political and security domain; for the Americans, the situation has produced no less pressing challenges to established expectations and institutions at home. In November 1991, the NATO summit in Rome saw even the US administration articulating some of the American questioning of the continued security link between a uniting Europe and the USA.[5]

This leads us to identify a third structural transformation: the increasing linkage of domestic with external events and processes, and the increasing political interpenetration of the two previously separate domains of 'economics' and 'security'. Such intersections have been notionally recognized since the 1970s if not before. The distinguishing feature of the 1990s is that the objective change in international and domestic conditions has been matched by a cognitive shift on the part of policy elites, which has led to the recognition of the new realities and which has at times led to the bewilderment of policymakers and their publics alike. This assessment reflects the fact that the cognitive shift, though fundamental and substantial, is not complete, nor has it been thoroughly incorporated into policy processes and political dialogue.

Although the politics of structural change, and the recognition of fundamental shifts by policymakers, are clearly at the root of many policy difficulties, it is important to examine the forms in which these difficulties arise. The first such category concerns the policy agenda. The case for structural change implies that both American and European policymakers are confronted with a transformed range of choices and issues. The notion, however, that everything has changed is profoundly misleading. The reality is a situation of differentiated and partial transformation; tensions thus arise from the varying rates and scopes of change in different areas of policy, and from the coexistence of the 'old' with the 'new' on the policy agenda. Traditionally, it might be argued, the dominant agenda in Atlantic relations has been that of military security, and that area has been itself dominated by the USA, with its nuclear predominance and its structural ascendancy in the alliance. It was not unaffected by changes in the economic sphere, but it assumed primacy over them, thanks not least to the role played by the USSR in Euro-Atlantic developments. The economic framework constituted by the GATT and the Bretton Woods system reflected American structural dominance, and the emergence of the EC as a major partner/competitor for the Americans took place within this structure, not as a challenge to it.[6]

This traditional view of the transatlantic agenda has been challenged for perhaps the past twenty years, not least by the changing behaviour of the Americans themselves. The shift from American 'guardianship' of the system to US ambivalence towards it can be fairly closely dated to the early 1970s. In the security sphere the overriding dominance of security in transatlantic relations was qualified by US–Soviet detente. In the economic sphere the US first moved to floating exchange rates and then, less dramatically but no less importantly, towards a more unilateral approach to trade policy as reflected in the 1974 US Trade Act. Notwithstanding such shifts, the emphasis during the 1970s and much of the 1980s was on the need for reform within the established concept of the policy agenda: a search for mechanisms and procedures which could make the Americans and the Europeans more aware of their changing priorities and which could accommodate the impact of a more turbulent global economic and security environment. At one level this could be cloaked in a certain idealism, while at another it represented an effort to limit the damage that could be caused by potentially uncontrolled change. The point made in discussion even during the Reagan years was not that the world had been transformed, but that there were sources of – often severe – strain within the established framework. Policymakers returned constantly to the need for amendment and adjustment, and were much occupied with pulling and hauling within the established structures and areas of contention.

The 1990s have challenged this view of the Atlantic policy agenda, fundamentally and pervasively. The origins can be found as far back as 1985, although even then they were perceived as issues within the existing agenda rather than about the relevance of the agenda itself. Since 1985, we have witnessed the disappearance of the established Soviet/ American security agenda; structural developments in the world economy and Atlantic economic relations brought about by the diffusion of economic power and by the more rapid communication that has resulted from technological advances; the rise of dynamic and continuing debates in both the United States and the Community about their nature as international actors and about their economic and security priorities. Intersecting these radical shifts have been a number of other develop- ments relating to North/South relations, to newly salient global issues such as those of environmental change and human rights, and to the relationship between regionalism and globalism in both economic and security concerns.

Linkage has become more important because the separation between the economic and the political or security elements of transatlantic relations has become effectively impossible either in intellectual or in policy terms. In the 1990s, there is no possibility of confining notions of economic partnership and security alliance to separate boxes. The intim- acy of the linkage between the two is well recognized in the debates about the 'peace dividend' and 'strategic technologies'. For both the USA and the EC, there is a well-documented if still debatable set of linkages between stability and prosperity, between welfare and potential warfare. What makes the 1990s different is the political recognition of this linkage, its novel status as the central focus of debate about national priorities, and the different ways in which this has made itself felt in the USA and Europe.

From the USA's point of view, a dominating feature of debate has been the need to redefine the balance between prosperity and security, and an attempt to introduce into the security arena considerations of competitiveness and industrial policy. For the EC, the process has been almost entirely the opposite, with the debate turning upon the ways in which a concern for security can be grafted onto the civilian power-base established through the traditional Community activities and institutions and achieved through the success of European economic integration. This is both influenced by and influences the EC's concept of security. For the Community, security certainly encompasses political stability and thus economic and social progress in its neighbours, especially those in central and eastern Europe, but it also extends to North/South and global environmental issues. A parallel process can be seen to be operating in US approaches to central and South America, either through the initiation of NAFTA to include Mexico or through such measures as the Enterprise for the Americas programme; but it might still be argued that the broader US conception of security retains the cold-war overtones of military priorities.[7]

The debates in the US and the EC cannot be insulated from each other: indeed, one of the dominating facts about the 'politics of linkage' in US/ EC relations is the interaction of what might be seen as purely 'domestic' debates and priorities with those of international concern. Given this intimate linkage between domestic and international for both the US and the EC, alongside the structural shifts already outlined, a major problem emerges: that of policy consistency, and the management of the linkages themselves. Henry Kissinger used to talk of the uses of linkages as if they could be manipulated and controlled by a central intelligence; it is now clear that the problem of linkage is as much one of the limits to knowledge and control as it is one of rational and systematic combination. This is particularly true for political and economic systems in which there is a high level of interpenetration and interdependence, such as those of the US and the EC.

Problems of policy consistency and control are ultimately problems of attention and communication: the capacity to give attention to different and often conflicting demands, and the ability to communicate reliably in conditions of considerable flux. No longer is it possible to rely on shared perceptions of interest shaped by the awareness of dominant conflicts and powers, as arguably was the case in the 1950s and 1960s. Despite attempts throughout the 1970s and 1980s to enhance communication between the two sides of the Atlantic, at both the bilateral and the multilateral level, the record betrays an increasing range of transatlantic disputes and uncertainties arising from events in nuclear policy, the management of the world economy, and regional conflicts such as those in Southeast Asia or the Middle East. Given the contextual factors discussed earlier, it is clear that the demands of the 1990s are a fundamental challenge to the control of policy and of interactions between interested parties. To put it crudely, while there is more need than ever for the identification both of shared interests and of clashing ones, conditions make it infinitely more difficult to do this than in the past. The demands of domestic audiences are pervasive: in the case of the Community, they are reflected particularly but not only in the tensions between national governments and the Community position; in the case of the US, the impact of fragmentation within the federal government and the growth of parochial interests has created a potent brew in many areas affecting external policy.[8]

One of the shaping factors in perceptions of common interest and the generation of common expectations is that of burden-sharing. As historically defined, the notion of burden-sharing has been applied particularly to the distribution of defence expenditures within the Atlantic alliance. In the 1990s a much broader definition is appropriate. It is possible, in fact, to trace a broad set of assumptions about the distribution of costs and benefits, of 'goods' and 'bads', back to the earliest years of postwar European/American relations; the trade-off between political stability, economic reconstruction, defence through the alliance and adherence to the multilateral economic framework has been a constant thread in the Euro-Atlantic system. If it appears novel in the 1990s, it is because the linkages between these areas have come much closer to the surface and have become politicized in an unprecedented way. Whereas contextual forces – the Soviet threat, the need for Western solidarity, the predominance of the USA – historically muted the redistributive pressures underlying the Euro-Atlantic system, such forces have now either been knocked away or been given a radically different meaning.

In this changed situation, the calculation for policymakers is essentially and qualitatively different from that of burden-sharing as traditionally defined, and the trade-offs are correspondingly more complex. We have moved from a situation in which the central fact was the defence predominance of the United States, and in which the burden-sharing debate was about how to divide the labour between the dominant and the subordinate members of the alliance, to a situation in which the definition of defence and security itself is open to question at both the national and the international level. Not only this, but we have entered a world in which the conflicting demands on policymakers for attention and resources have no settled rank-order, and in which politicization is endemic. When it comes to the notion of a redefined Euro-Atlantic partnership for the 1990s and beyond, one of the key questions needing an answer is whether such a partnership constitutes a good, or even a necessary, investment *per se*. Policymakers today have far fewer reliable parameters to guide them in such a calculation.

Related to the concept of burden-sharing is that of institutional frameworks, and by implication institutional choices. When the Euro-Atlantic partnership of the 1950s was established, it was alongside a broader institutional network which expressed the structural centrality both of the Atlantic alliance and of the United States within the international arena. The situation of the 1990s is very different, and the transformation of the institutional context is both a support to and a hindrance for policy. Because the setting is what might be described as 'institution-rich', policymakers can take advantage of a range of institutional supports for any given line of action. At the same time, however, they are not only constrained by the requirements of the institutions concerned but daunted by the sheer range of possible channels through which to work. In the same way as linkages pose problems of attention and priority, so do coexisting and sometimes competing institutional frameworks. Arguably also, the recognized decline of the USA's ability to impose or influence choices of institutional contexts has created new tensions and gaps which can be exploited. Practical examples abound: in dealing with trade and industrial policies, should priority be given to global organizations such as the GATT, or to more narrowly regional or bilateral mechanisms such as the EC or NAFTA? In confronting the need for assistance to the former Soviet Union, which is the appropriate coordinating agency: the International Monetary Fund (IMF), the European Bank for Reconstruction and Development (EBRD), the EC or the Group of Seven industrial countries (G7)? In dealing with issues of security narrowly defined, which is the first resort: the UN (United Nations), NATO (North Atlantic Treaty Organization), the CSCE (Conference on Security and Cooperation in Europe), or other regional, sub-regional and national bodies, including the EC?

As the Atlantic Declaration of November 1990 shows, there is also scope for the development of new transatlantic institutional channels. Now that the EC has moved some way towards defining its own role in foreign and security policy at Maastricht, the debate on transforming the declaration into a treaty could well re-emerge. But if such a transformation were to take place, the new institutional arrangements would necessarily be influenced by the existing dense and diverse institutional array outlined here. No less will it be influenced by the fact that the US and the EC, or European countries individually, must also cooperate with other important players, often on a bilateral basis. On security issues this includes the successor states of the Soviet Union as well as countries such as China. In the economic domain it includes many countries but above all Japan.[9]

Another institution that has found some application in recent years as a place in which to coordinate the roles of the key players – among them the US and the EC – is that of the G7 summit meetings. The issue here is less what the G7 can itself do – opposition to a *directoire* from France among others restricts this in any case – but more whether it can be used for coordination of actions taken by the participants in other institutional settings and thus provide some form of rudimentary burden-sharing between the economic and security fields. As in the case of a possible Transatlantic Treaty, the role of an enhanced G7 would inevitably be shaped by the depth and intensity of existing institutionalization among industrial countries.

Any attempt to redefine Euro-Atlantic relations for the 1990s thus has to confront the proliferation of channels and devices, the potential for competition between them, and the equally significant potential for gaps when it comes to unexpected and challenging developments. Not least must it confront the ambiguities of status attending US/EC relations. On the one side, there is the acknowledged predominant power, but a power with important reservations and uncertainties about its international role. On the other, there is the potential power, with no formal representation in a multitude of the most salient organizations and a need to act in many cases by proxy or consensus if it is to make its collective will felt.

For European/American relations, this means that there are important questions about the 'rules of the game' and political practice in the 1990s. There has always been difficulty in this area: from the beginning of the 1950s, the issue of American leadership and West European 'followership' has bedevilled notions of partnership. Alongside this, there has been a problem of procedures and consultation, which has often taken the form of American unilateralism and European recriminations, but which has been accompanied by privileged bilateral relationships between Washington and national capitals. The most obvious instance of this problem is that of the 'special relationship' between the United States and Britain, but it has not been the only one. In a sense, given the structural context for

US/European relations, there has been a series of 'special relationships' between the USA and all West European countries, with different links becoming salient at different times. As Chapter 4 shows, the importance of the US/German (and the weakness of the US/French) relationship was a feature of Euro-American relations in the 1990–91 period. A final aspect of the general problem is that of leverage, given that the broad distribution of power within the Euro-Atlantic partnership has never fully predicted the outcomes of specific disputes or tensions. The expectation that American wishes would prevail in all areas of dispute has always been suspect, either because of failures of American policy or will, or because of the ability of specific Europeans to resist and channel American pressures.[10]

These three issues – of partnership and privilege, of procedures and of leverage – have a new salience in the transformed conditions of the 1990s, and as a result have important implications for policymakers. The removal or rebalancing of major structural features has created a situation in which the broad expectations outlined above can no longer be sustained, but in which no reliable substitute can be found for them. American leadership can be and has been challenged, not least by Americans themselves, but there is as yet no clear answer to the questions 'who leads' or 'should there be leadership'? The assertion of unilateralism, and the creation of privileged relationships, have been issues throughout the 1980s, but there has emerged no clear redefinition of the procedures through which Euro-Atlantic relations might work. This, of course, reflects the institutional diversity outlined above, but there is no denying its impact at the level of policy choices and priorities. To cite just one example, the problems of dealing with a newly predominant Germany in the context of a changing Europe have preoccupied Americans and Europeans alike. The exertion of effective leverage (or, for that matter, of ineffective leverage) remains an area of dispute and uncertainty among Atlantic countries, and is given entirely new dimensions by the proliferation of 'targets' in the former Soviet Union and eastern Europe, with their implications for interests and attention.

Towards a new Euro-Atlantic partnership?
This chapter has outlined a number of the most significant elements working to transform the context for Euro-Atlantic relations, and has attempted to relate them in general terms to policy issues and choices confronting both Americans and Europeans. What is the burden of the general argument?

First, the changes affecting Euro-Atlantic relations are radical and structural rather than marginal or conjunctural. This is at its most apparent in the context of the former Soviet Union and eastern Europe, but it is none the less significant as regards the development of the world economy. A key feature of the changes is that they have become recognized as such, and that the governing consensus among western policymakers has internalized them. In other words, there is not only a substantive component to the issues but a cognitive one.

Second, there are a number of areas in which the radical, structural and cognitive changes have thrown up policy problems. One of these is the growth of complex linkages with multiple points of intersection. Although a good part of the problem here is centred upon Euro-Atlantic relations themselves, it is apparent that the centrality of those relations in the changing global arena can be disputed, and that the capacity to set the agenda is not solely a function of what goes on between Washington and European capitals.

Two further implications of the growth of linkages have been highlighted: the increasingly complex linkage between the economic and the security domains, and the interpenetration of 'domestic' and 'international' concerns. The net effect of these two trends has been to create a growing politicization of external affairs in both the United States and the EC, fed by the perception that what goes on at home conditions and is conditioned by change on the other side of the Atlantic and in the world at large. This is not a new discovery; but the combination of these factors with the structural shifts identified earlier is of the utmost importance to both the United States and the Community.

On the basis of these shifts and trends, it is possible to argue that a number of long-standing transatlantic issues have a radically new meaning and impact. The nature, identification and communication of common interests is both more crucial and more difficult than before. The notion of burden-sharing has a new scope, and the calculation of costs and benefits in Atlantic relations is more complex and more politicized than ever. An institution-rich transatlantic arena poses problems of attention, coordination and priorities. The legitimacy and efficacy of processes of consultation, and the relative salience of bilateral and multilateral relationships, is challenged by change but has not been conclusively redefined. Large questions of coordination and cooperation remain to be recognized, let alone tackled, and their handling will be crucial to the necessary redefinition of Euro-Atlantic relations.

Change and challenge are thus radical, but they are not unconstrained by the past or by existing structures and patterns. It is not open to either the United States or the Community to act as if nothing had gone before. Redefinition cannot start with a blank sheet, and this raises an important area for exploration. It is possible, not to say probable, that the redefinition has started to take shape and that the components of a new Euro-Atlantic partnership are lying around waiting to be assembled into a new and seemingly designed whole. The catalyst for this new recognition and act of creation is as yet undiscovered, or at least unrecognized, but it is important to open the debate about the elements it will need to combine.

2

DOMESTIC PREOCCUPATIONS AND INTERNATIONAL IDENTITIES

During the past five years, the domestic and international identities of both the European Community and the US have been subject to extensive redefinition. This process is incomplete and so far inconclusive in both cases, but it exerts a profound influence upon the ways in which both Americans and Europeans approach the problems of domestic governance and international life. As such, it is a vital source of evidence and argument when it comes to discussion of a potential redefinition for the Euro-Atlantic system.

What are the key areas in which this redefinition and search for identity has taken effect? We argue that there are three:

(1) Both the US and the EC have been engaged in essentially 'domestic' debates about the economic and political structures through which they can best express the aspirations of their citizens in a changing world. These debates about the forms and functions of governance have taken different forms and expressions on the two sides of the Atlantic, but they have immense significance for the relations between the two entities.

(2) A major focus of debate and contention in both the US and the EC has been the policymaking process and the role of government in a changing world context. In many ways, this is an extension of the 'domestic' debates outlined above, but it has focused attention sharply on institutions and priorities, albeit again in different ways in the two cases.

(3) The debates in the US and the EC are conditioned by the increasing and intense policy interdependence between the two entities. The

14

Community is thus an element in the US 'domestic' debate, and the US is a component of the Community process. Often, this 'presence' is implicit rather than explicit, but the interpenetration of the US and the EC at many levels creates a high level of mutual sensitivity with the potential for frictions and unintended outcomes.

Exploration of these areas is thus an essential starting-point for later discussion of the ways in which the US and the Community have responded to the challenges of the 1990s, and in which they might forge a new partnership for the rest of the century and beyond. The chapter will explore, first, the debates and developments in the US and the EC, and then the ways in which these intersect within the international arena.

The United States: dominance and disillusion
The domestic and international politics of the USA have constituted a major unsolved problem of international order since the late 1960s. Although there has been nothing remotely to match the traumatic events in the former Soviet sphere, Americans have none the less been faced with the question 'what kind of USA?' in an often sharp and insistent form and over an extended period. As a result, the 'American identity' has been a source of ambivalence both for American policy elites and for those – such as the EC and its members – with whom they have had to deal. The internal American debates about 'decline' and the changing nature of American power have generated not only a copious literature but also a persistent set of tensions within and outside the policy machine; although the problems may have taken different forms under the successive presidencies from Nixon to Bush, they have expressed the same essential dilemmas and pressures.[1]

In common with other industrial societies, the United States has increasingly experienced the effects of 'penetrated' or 'perforated' sovereignty as interdependence has increased. In addition, it has been recognized both in the USA and elsewhere that many aspects of policy are multi-layered, creating problems of 'boundary definition' and 'boundary control' not only within society but also between national jurisdictions and the outside world. This set of relationships has been a central feature of the American domestic scene during the past decade, and it has become a pressing issue in the context of demands for both economic and political revitalization. The fact is that increasingly the 'American model' of social and economic development is open to question both at home and abroad. At home, the concerns centre on worries about whether the US model of free market capitalism can, in the long run, compete with Japan or Germany and thus provide a basis for US strength. Abroad, it is no longer the case that the US is seen as the model of prosperity. The alternative European (see below) or Japanese 'models' have now gained equal if not greater credibility. The European approach to dealing with increased interdependence of economies or interpenetration of societies has, in particular, gained credibility thanks to the progress in European integration during the 1980s and poses a challenge for the US in international negotiations. This loss of confidence in the US 'model' constitutes a basic input into the Euro-Atlantic future.[2]

In which areas have the problems made themselves most painfully felt? Perhaps the most public debates and evidence have occurred in the area of industrial structure and industrial policies. There has been an intense concern at many levels in the USA with competitiveness, innovation and the preservation of the American position in the industrial hierarchy. In areas such as semiconductors, consumer electronics, automobiles and aerospace, the American landscape and political debate provide a full range of 'symptoms': penetration of US sovereignty, perceptions of industrial rivalry, attempts to respond through consortium arrangements between indigenous US firms and through managed trade. Closely linked to this area is that of military-industrial structure: the area in which the intersection of concern with national security and industrial strength has created a growing paranoia about the threat to strategic sectors or enterprises. Such pressures as these have been visible since the early 1970s: they assumed a central and paradoxical importance during the Reagan years, and they continued to plague the Bush presidency. The traditionally non-interventionist approach of the US will no doubt prevail in the short term, but the calls for explicit forms of industrial policy rather than covert use of defence expenditure have grown, and no longer emanate exclusively from the Democratic Party in election years.

The impact of global political change and the promise of the 'peace dividend' has thus been especially paradoxical, since for a long time the defence industrial base has been one of the more dynamic elements of the economy; removal of the cold-war imperative has exposed the nerves of a rather fragile and unresponsive industrial structure. It may be considered a source of strength that the American economy can respond to the imperatives of global economic change, but there is no doubt also that the process of response has aroused perceptions of weakness and demands for defensive measures.[3]

Problems of industrial structure have been compounded by their intersection with those of the financial structure. Increasingly, this has given evidence of domestic fragility and vulnerability to outside forces, and there has been growing debate about the relevance or effectiveness of regulatory structures in the USA. The 'double deficits' brought on by the lax fiscal and monetary policies of the 1980s, and accentuated by the inability of Congress and the administration to agree on a viable policy to contain them, have merely underlined some persistent structural weaknesses. The shift from being a net lender to being a significant debtor country is one manifestation of the structural change which has occurred. Politically, these new realities have found expression in the mounting concern with the impact of foreign investment, even though the double deficit necessitates continued inflows of capital, including Japanese capital. Regulatory failures, such as in the Savings and Loans case, combined with excessive credit-based growth, such as that driven by 'junk bonds' during the 1980s, are stretching the resources of federal and state agencies to breaking-point by demands for supervision and bail-outs. In 1991, Congress failed yet again to respond by passing comprehensive reforms sought by banks and regulators alike. The failure of banking reforms, and the immense difficulties faced by the financial system in general, have heightened the perception of transnational threats and the inadequacies of domestic financial and political institutions.

Confidence in the long-term prospects for the US economy has also been hit by the problems in the educational system, especially in the cities, and by a general deterioration of the physical and social infrastructure of the country. As in previous pre-election periods, this domestic agenda has been promoted by critics of the incumbent administration, but during 1991–2 there was a broad recognition that the US faces serious domestic structural problems. Therefore, at the same time as the 'triumph of democracy' was being trumpeted on the basis of events in the Soviet Union, eastern Europe and the Gulf, there has been a growing insecurity about the efficacy of capitalist democracy on the home front – a further challenge to the American 'model'.

This suggests that a 'third deficit' has arisen, relating to the declining credibility and legitimacy of government. The overwhelming perception is of inadequacies at the federal level which have led to a disillusionment with politics and politicians and which have thus eroded the legitimacy of the political system in general. At the level of the American state authorities there has been a trend towards innovation in economic policies and international activities, exemplified by the growth of state-based

17

international economic policies targeted at the EC and Japan; but even these are surrounded by evidence of financial and political tension. Indeed, a number of commentators have openly suggested the existence of a social and cultural crisis in the USA, arising from diverse sources but magnified by the failings of government at several levels, and the history of H. Ross Perot's intervention in the 1992 election campaign can be seen as symbolizing a deep-seated distrust of American government in general.[4]

Another structural issue, and one which has a specific resonance for the study of Euro-Atlantic relations, is the shifting centre of gravity in US political and economic life. Throughout the 1980s, it was noted that the rise of the South and the West constituted a major feature of the changing political landscape. Although in this respect George Bush might be seen as a bit of a political throwback – a classical example of the East Coast elite, despite his mock-Texan origins – it is incontestable that the dominance of the East Coast establishment, and of the classic industrial base centred on the East and the Middle West, has been eroded. The domestic perception that economic stakes are highest and the threat most immediate in relation to the Pacific rather than the Atlantic is an important adjunct to this shift; President Bush's ill-fated oriental tour in early 1992 betrayed both the strength of the perception and its permeation of the American political system, and the lack of any settled views about how to deal with it. At the same time, the moves towards a North American Free Trade Area bringing in Mexico, and the continuation of the Enterprise for the Americas Initiative, have underlined the southern as well as the western elements of the new US position.[5]

Three conclusions follow from this brief discussion. First, domestic structure is a matter of acute political concern and acute political dilemma in the United States of the 1990s. Second, this concern with domestic structure cannot be divorced from developments in the international arena; in fact, in many cases there is an intimate organic link between domestic uncertainties and international challenges, with one feeding off the other. Finally, this linkage reflects a secular decline in the insulation of the USA from the global arena, and in the insulation of specific sectors of US political, economic and social life from each other. The linkages between federal, state, regional and local processes are changing; so are those between public and private interests and policymaking, as are those between the economic, the political and the security interests of American society; and all of them are penetrated by the integration of the American economy and society into the global arena, which means that the pace of change in domestic structures, however rapid, may not be rapid enough to match increasing international demands. As we shall argue later, the EC is implicated in this process in a number of ways, and the nature of 'Europe' has become a datum of the debate within American society.

Alongside the issues raised by domestic structure, a constant concern of the past twenty years has been the policymaking process in the USA. There has been no point since the early 1960s at which the American public has had complete confidence in national policymaking or policymakers, and the fluctuating debate about the credentials and legitimacy of the policy machine has formed a leitmotif for much of the past decade. The Bush administration came to office at a time when the policymaking process at federal level had been subject to a decade and more of critical attention, the Reagan years having raised a questioning of the control and execution of policies that amounted, some argued, to an 'unmaking' of the policy machine. The Reagan years also saw a transfer of power back to the states. This may have helped ease the problem of the 'third deficit' of governmental credibility, but in a range of areas it accentuated the problems of linkage between domestic and foreign economic policy. As Chapter 3 shows, for example, increased interdependence touches state-level policies, creating significant difficulties when it comes to negotiating multilateral agreements for investment and regulatory policies. One of the key promises made by George Bush during the 1988 election campaign was a 'remaking' of policy, with coherence and continuity as the keynotes, but it is still open to question whether the changing structure of US government will allow this to extend to many areas of regulation and economic or social policy. Alongside all of the novel features there persists the Democrat dominance in the Congress, which is a source of constraint and possible tensions despite the attempts of the Bush administration to conciliate.[6]

The Bush administration's programme thus faced severe obstacles from the outset, some of them emerging directly from the domestic forces outlined earlier and from the legacy of Reaganism. Whatever the talents and the experience of the administration, it faced a multi-layered and complex policy arena, a fast-developing agenda and problems connected with US status and leverage in the global system. None the less, the Bush presidency developed a distinctive policymaking style in which the experience and 'hands-on' approach of the President himself formed a striking contrast to the Reagan years. A strong emphasis was laid on personal contacts between the President and other leaders, and there was an equally strong trend towards a policy process based on 'networking' between a group of professionals in any given instance or sector, such as the team gathered by James Baker at the State Department. What this achieved was sensitivity to new developments; what it might have sacrificed is the notion of policy design and coherence, given the apparent gap between the micro-level of personal diplomacy and the broad-brush setting-out of concepts such as the 'New World Order', which will be assessed later. The evidence from a number of episodes, including those in eastern Europe and the Pacific region, is that a policy gap of this kind does exist, and that the presidency itself is not always able to bridge it.[7]

To this broad need for enhanced policy control at home has been added the demand for international policy coordination – a demand dramatically illustrated by the Gulf war coalition, but none the less significant in areas such as trade and macroeconomic policymaking. Domestically, policy control of economic – and especially trade – issues is made all the more difficult by the number and diversity of constituencies affected and the constitutional role of Congress in determining commercial policy. Where Congress itself is at odds both internally and with the President on a wide range of issues, the search for external coordination is made all the more difficult, and this will be explored in Chapters 3 and 4.

What was the Bush administration's response to these actually or potentially conflicting demands on its attention and its capacity for coordination? One response was exceptionally clear: a tendency to articulate new ways of dealing with allies and adversaries, and to search for the bases on which international coalitions might be constructed. Speeches by the President and Secretary of State Baker can be seen to have had a strong programmatic element (as for example in the cases of the 'New World Order', the new 'Euro-Atlantic architecture' and later the 'Euro-Atlantic community'). No opportunity was missed to try to shape the agenda of allied and other relations, or to build on coincidences of interest in the hope of arriving at deals between the most committed of adversaries. The Secretary of State in particular proved adept at using momentum in such situations as the Arab/Israeli conflict to create negotiating contexts. There is no doubt that in this respect there were important contrasts with the insularity of many Reaganite policy initiatives. The question, though, is what follow-through can there be once the situations have been created? In this case, the issue of US leverage is highly relevant, and will be dealt with below.[8]

Another striking feature of the Bush policy stance, at least until the beginning of 1992 (and the election campaign), was a major disjunction between foreign and domestic policy. Indeed, it would not be going too far to see the Bush administration as a paradigm of the 'two presidencies' case, with a stark contrast between the freedom of action, the attention and the prestige seen as attaching to foreign policy and the constraints and obstacles encountered in domestic policy. The contrast has in effect been central to presidencies from Lyndon Johnson's onwards, often with damaging political consequences, but the nature of international and domestic change in the late 1980s and 1990s has underlined its potential for intervention in the political fates of American leaders. Quite simply, whatever the preferences of presidents or their administrations, domestic political and economic issues are difficult and inescapable.

Perhaps as a reflection of this contrast, by the beginning of 1992 it was clear that a major and damaging gap had emerged between the enthusiasm and energy devoted to foreign policy and the neglect – benign or otherwise – characterizing domestic activity. At times, it appeared that the White House and the State Department existed in a cocoon of 'high diplomacy' unconnected with even the most substantial and pressing of other demands. This is particularly significant given the interconnectedness of many foreign and domestic concerns, and some painful awakenings to this linkage were apparent during 1991. On a number of 'intermestic' issues, where international and domestic pressures intersect, the Congress had a good deal of latitude while the administration appeared distracted; in such cases of neglect, congressional, state and corporate interests had more of a voice than the administration itself (for example, on industrial policy concerns or on some issues relating to the 1992 Earth summit in Rio de Janeiro). In this respect, the conditions replicated those of 1987–8, when the Reagan administration's benign neglect of domestic issues came home to roost and played an influential role in the election campaign. The 1992 election campaign has had a similar effect by compelling the President to dirty his hands with domestic concerns (a conclusion borne out by the January 1992 State of the Union address, but then underlined more dramatically by unrest in Los Angeles and elsewhere); but there was none the less a tendency to use external activity for domestic effect. The President's Japan mission of January 1992 proved the dangers of attempting to turn over a new leaf with the old methods, and of using foreign policy for domestic economic and political ends: the administration appeared on the one hand to be playing to the parochial audience, but on the other to be outflanked by the ability of the Japanese to resist or to turn trade policy pressures to their advantage.[9]

In general, the Bush administration placed a good deal of emphasis in

21

policymaking on communication and atmosphere, but this is not always enough to ensure the effective attainment of policy objectives. Even in 'success stories', such as the Gulf war, the consequences of achieving one set of aims entailed further hard work, often with intractable adversaries or allies, to move on to the next stage. Trade policy issues, albeit less dramatic, displayed some of the same features. Perhaps not surprisingly, the administration appeared at times to be neither in control of domestic events nor fully in tune with international trends – stuck increasingly in a kind of no man's land of positions without implementation or leverage, and with only a limited capacity to pay detailed attention to a diverse policy agenda. Whether it was the Middle East peace talks, the provision of aid to the former Soviet Union, or the ability to agree within the GATT Uruguay Round, the gap between position and action persisted. When it came to the redefinition of American/European relations, such limitations of policymaking were likely to be crucial, and we have to ask whether any successors to the Bush administration would be able to escape them.[10]

Where does US policy go from here? The one certain prognostication in 1992 is that domestic electoral politics will play a central role in shaping American positions both in the economic and in the security order. But the domestic scene itself is turbulent and fragmented, with warring concepts of social and political regeneration coming to the fore in the context of a continuing recession. During the early part of 1992, the maverick candidacy of H. Ross Perot for the presidency captured much of this turbulence, demonstrating the mercurial nature of the US political scene. The 'lonely superpower' appears more distracted and preoccupied than at any time during the past decade – perhaps more than at any time since the Vietnam trauma. As noted earlier, one possible longer-term consequence will be a kind of 'ratchet effect', leaving the next American president with an agenda determined by commitments made for domestic purposes, both in the economic and in the security domain. The restoration of 'normal politics' between the Bush and Clinton camps after the apparent demise of the Perot campaign in mid-1992 does not detract from the strength of this assessment, and the reappearance of the 'Perot factor' in late 1992 only reinforced it. Meanwhile, on the other side of the Atlantic, a very different kind of superpower may be in the making.

The European Community: new model superpower?
One of the most frequently repeated assertions about the international role of the EC is that it does not convert its economic weight and

dynamism into effective political action. It does not 'punch its weight'; it is an 'economic giant and a political pygmy'; it shelters behind the position that it is a 'civilian power' which does not, and by implication should not, possess the full range of international political and security capacities. Development and debate during the past three years, though, has given cause for revision if not yet definitive judgments. The EC, post-Maastricht, possesses the apparent basis for effective action going beyond the Treaty of Rome and far beyond the purely 'civilian' domain. But the argument in this area is only just beginning, even leaving aside the uncertainties about ratification of Maastricht as a result of the Danish referendum of June 1992 and the doubts reflected in the narrow result of the French referendum in September; the purpose here is to investigate the Community's credentials as an international actor as they are likely to affect its relations with the USA during the mid-1990s. A major part of this investigation is directed not only towards the Community's formal 'constitutional' position, as set out in the treaties and their extension to common foreign and security policy in Maastricht, but also towards its self-definition and the expectations created by the continuing debate over European Union.[11]

The dominating concern of Community policymaking and politics during the late 1980s was the regeneration of its industrial structure. The objective of the single European market (SEM) programme was to overcome the structural weakness of the European economy stemming from the fragmentation of the European market between national markets, and thus to enhance the competitiveness of European industry and revitalize the European economy. Momentum for change came both from markets and from Community policies: the former was backed by powerful industrial lobbies, operating as much in a global as in an exclusively European context. Policy-led integration came in the shape of, among other things, the 1986 Single European Act, which introduced qualified majority voting for internal market measures. There has always been a tension within the EC between the desire to promote competition by removing non-tariff barriers to national markets, and the desire for cooperation through joint projects, such as the collaborative R&D programmes, as a means of enhancing competitiveness. At the same time, there have been tensions between the desire to liberate through deregulation and the push for greater Community competence and activism.

In a number of important ways, the SEM programme thus underlined the well-established view of the Community as a predominantly economic concern, with politics entering the scene only through the back door. By taking as its cue the completion of the Treaty of Rome commitments, and by delaying consideration of enlargement until after 1992, the programme reinforced not only the 'civilian' nature of the Community but also the perception that it would flourish on the basis of exclusion and privilege. If that seems a harsh judgment, it should be remembered that one of the most fundamental elements in the EC's creation and growth was the division of Europe and the insulation of economics from security. The SEM programme, though, inevitably created a momentum which threatened to overspill these boundaries. On the one hand, it embodied an attempt to regenerate European industry, and was thus seen by non-Europeans or non-participants as threatening and potentially discriminatory. Hence the emergence of the 'fortress Europe' debate; at the same time, the push for greater integration fostered developments, for example in defence-related industries, which raised questions about the boundaries of Commission competence and Community presence. On the other hand, the very success of the SEM programme in raising expectations and generating momentum acted as a magnet for outside countries, especially those in the European Free Trade Area (EFTA), and equally fostered a new vitality in the interest of multinational corporate actors.[12]

The logic of the SEM programme did not stop with industrial goods; indeed, the Cockfield White Paper of 1985 included provisions to liberalize financial markets and thus to enhance monetary and financial integration. Economic and monetary union (EMU) has been on the Community agenda since the end of the Bretton Woods system of fixed exchange rates, and the SEM programme, combined with the decision to free all capital movements within the EC, set the scene for the initiation of the latest attempt in June 1988. The preparation for negotiations about economic and monetary union was thus well under way before the shockwaves of change in eastern Europe hit the Community. Alongside this, the increasing recognition of a 'European economic space', based on the interaction of the Community and its EFTA neighbours, had produced debate not only about the desirability of such a space but about its form and functioning. In these ways the developments between 1987 and 1989 led to a partial transformation of the Community's international identity, almost without this being explicitly on the Community's agenda.[13]

The fall of the Berlin Wall and events surrounding it produced crucial additional pressures and provided the catalyst for intense debate about the Community's internal and external structure. In the first place, the move to unification in Germany and the transformation of regimes in eastern Europe attacked some of the central premises underlying the 'classical'

Community. The new situation generated an intense linkage between the economic development of the EC and its political structure, by putting onto the agenda the question of how to contain a 'new Germany', and how to adjust to the new weight of the Community's largest member. At the same time, it lent new urgency to the connection between internal completion of the SEM programme and external relations with the rest of Europe, especially the new democracies in central and eastern Europe.[14]

As a result, the emphasis in the Community's internal politics and internal structure shifted profoundly during 1990 – a shift which found formal expression in the Maastricht agreement in December 1991. The initial product of this shift was the addition of a second intergovernmental conference on European political union (EPU) to that already agreed on EMU, and an acceleration of the EMU negotiations. Although the ostensible purpose of the EPU process was the creation of a new proto-federal structure for the Community, the underlying message was that of political adaptation to the changing centre of gravity in Europe. This is not to argue that the intense national and Community debates about subsidiarity and sovereignty (initially more intense in the United Kingdom than elsewhere) should be ignored; rather, we would contend that the need to accommodate and to contain the 'new Germany', and the need to reflect the linkages between the SEM programme and the new politics of Europe, lent urgency and dynamism to the process. What this also means is that the process is not by any means complete: Maastricht is a way-station, not a terminus, and the real nature, and thus the international implications, of the structures agreed, especially those concerning common foreign and security policy, are still to be resolved. The events of spring and summer 1992, when the Danish referendum served as a catalyst for doubts and uncertainties elsewhere in the Community, demonstrated that the domestic politics of the process would be a central feature. With economic burdens increasing while the capacities of national governments are placed under intense scrutiny, the mid-1990s promise to be a period of intense self-examination both for the EC and for its members.[15]

'Domestic' governance and political structure is thus as much of an issue for the Community as it is for the United States during the 1990s, albeit in very different ways. In fact, we would argue that it is a much more pressing and potentially crucial issue, given its relationship to the politics not only of the Community itself and its member states but of the surrounding continent as well. This uncovers another central feature of the situation: the difficulty for the Community of drawing the boundary between itself and the outside world. From the outset, it was artificial and misleading to contend that the SEM programme could take effect in isolation; it was always quintessentially an international programme, with international effects. When the SEM programme was joined on the agenda by EMU and EPU, this raised in urgent form the question of the Community's response to the changing international order, and demanded that the EC and its members decide on the balance between change and continuity. Although much attention has rightly been paid to these aspects of the Community's role in East/West relations, there is also an emerging 'North/South' dimension to change in Europe, which cannot fail to engage the Community itself, whether in the specific context of moves towards enlargement or in the more general light of concerns about social and economic stability in countries such as those bordering on the Mediterranean.[16]

A final 'domestic' element in the EC's self-redefinition is thus to be found in social structure and social consensus. Over the years the Community has not always been looked on as an island of stability and consensus in a turbulent world; indeed, one of the key features of its early years was the instability and fragility of key members such as France. In 1990, however, it appeared to some that the 'European model' of the social market economy and social partnership had finally come to fruition, and that this would in some way provide a beacon to the rest of Europe if not the world. At the same time the model has been subject to increasing strains arising from the turbulence of the new Europe and wider problems of the world economy. As already noted, the capacities of government and national state structures have come under scrutiny, with some of the sharpest questions being asked of those which had appeared most stable, such as Italy and the Federal Republic of Germany.

Alongside the increasing turbulence of the economic and political order, the 'new agenda' of environmental, humanitarian and welfare issues flowing from relations with its eastern and southern neighbours has increasingly had its impact on the Community, not least through the pressures it exerts on national and regional authorities. In this respect, there is a parallel to the growth of 'intermestic' policy issues and debates in the USA. To take perhaps the most dramatic and potentially traumatic example, problems of immigration and citizenship have acquired new intensity and political salience in the 1990s. For the Community, as for the USA, the issue of access – not only to markets but also to the benefits of society more generally – has thus become an agenda item of increasing sensitivity. The intersection of such concerns with the political instability and conflicts of the Balkans in particular has given the matter a sense not merely of urgency but even of desperation.[17]

In parallel with this process of 'domestic' structural change and redefinition, and at times as an integral part of it, there has been a significant development of the Community's policymaking processes. As already noted, the SEM programme could be seen as a policy response to the demands of increased economic interpenetration and market integration. More recently the Maastricht agreements focused strongly on the process as well as the substance of the EC's internal development. Subject to ratification of the European union treaty agreed in December 1991, the institutional context for Community decisionmaking will undergo important elaboration, with the creation of new organs such as the European Monetary Institute (EMI) and later the European Central Bank (ECB), and the redefinition of relationships between existing bodies, particularly the Commission, the Parliament and the Council. To be sure, there are anomalies and variations in the treaties, particularly those relating to the British position, but we would argue that these are largely apparent rather than real. The treaties on the whole confirm the increasing role of the EC in the monetary field, they open up important new areas of policymaking with the introduction of a common foreign and security policy and they extend or enhance EC competence on environmental and social issues. Many of these developments are in train independently of any doubts about the precise ratification process for Maastricht.

It is not our purpose here to go into detail about the results of Maastricht, but rather to draw out some factors which reflect a redefinition of the EC's internal and external evolution. One such factor is the increasing recognition of multi-layered policymaking in the Community. This is reflected in the notion of subsidiarity, and is an explicit recognition of the growth of regional government and of transnational as well as supranational networks in the Community. The multi-layered nature of policymaking is also reflected in the continued role for national governments and the 'balance of power' in the Community alongside the process of integration. As already noted, this found expression in the response of some countries to the 'new Germany'; within Germany itself, the often intense debate post-Maastricht about the powers and roles of the Länder has given further evidence of the differentiation between levels of policymaking and influence.[18]

Community policymaking is also being more effectively penetrated by forces originating outside the EC. One of the perennial arguments about EC policymaking concerns its openness or closedness, and the ability of its institutions to shut themselves away from the world outside. Among others, American administrations have had frequent cause to object to this tendency. This is partly an internal problem, and we have already noted that Maastricht implies an extension of Community activities into areas where many different social and economic groupings have a presence. More widely, though, it is apparent that a wide range of external forces now enter into EC decision processes. In the case of the EFTA countries, the situation is formalized. In the case of links with Western European Union (WEU) under the foreign and security policy umbrella, it cannot be taken for granted that the Community will assume the dominant and initiating role. Many other agreements with the countries of eastern Europe and elsewhere imply a legitimation of 'foreign' participants in EC processes. Meanwhile, those outsiders that were most concerned about gaining access to EC decisionmaking – including the United States – have managed to get their message across, and this includes non-governmental as well as governmental bodies. Although the Community may well remain predominantly a regional actor in the global arena, this does not prevent it being penetrated and suffused by the actions and influence of external groupings.[19]

The net result is a Community policymaking process which is increasingly if somewhat unevenly penetrated, and which gives sources of leverage to new participants. While the institutional balance in the Community itself has shifted perceptibly but not decisively in the context of Maastricht, the truly novel feature of the situation is a new context for coalition-building, negotiation and balance-of-power politics, influenced by a range of forces from within and outside the Community itself. The process of negotiation leading up to Maastricht, and the ways in which it intersected with the negotiations for the European Economic Area, the Uruguay Round and agreements with east European countries, demonstrate the complex coexistence of the dynamics of integration with the pressures of global and regional politics.

The Community has thus almost willy-nilly acquired a new decisionmaking style, which must take into account the voices not only of Community institutions and member governments, but also of other Europeans. At the same time, the Maastricht mechanisms seek to increase the effective coordination of different areas of Community activity, by reinforcing the link between commercial and monetary policies, and by confirming the development of links between Community policy and national foreign and security activities. Whilst Community members will still speak with their own national voices, these voices may be brought into closer harmony in so far as the Maastricht measures on common foreign and security policy are implemented. Often, there will be a firmer and more assertive Community voice backed up by agreements which may appear procedural but which have increasingly substantive implications. At the same time, the shifting balance of forces within the Community, between member states and between institutions, will play a significant role in conditioning the message and the channels through which it is expressed. Events surrounding the recognition of Slovenia and Croatia in early 1992 (see Chapter 4) thus give much cause for reflection on the process of EC policy formation, since they exposed the ways in which national and Community priorities could intersect or conflict. Other issues such as those of arms transfers promise some of the same tensions, given the Maastricht provisions for EC-level controls and the persistence of national variations in both the controls themselves and their effectiveness.

The analysis here of the European Community suggests a number of ambiguities and areas of tension, which are far from having been resolved by the agreements of Maastricht. The Community has been engaged in an extended process of self-redefinition, focused primarily on aspects of internal governance, but this process has been profoundly influenced by developments in the broader global economic and security orders as well as in US policies. The redefinition process is at least as much psychological as it is procedural or substantive, and the external impact of the process is at least as much in terms of expectations as in terms of tangible measures or actions. There are important if sometimes muted tensions between widening and deepening in the Community, between national, regional and global concerns and between an 'open' and 'closed' Community orientation. The Community's stance in the aftermath of Maastricht, and its increasing magnetism within Europe, might be described as 'expansive regionalism', but thereby hangs a series of highly sensitive political questions about the nature of the 'new Europe' and the Community's role within it.

The United States, the European Community and the world arena

In Chapter 1, we identified three key elements in the transformation of the world arena during the 1990s: radical structural change and the growth of linkages, the pressures for and the difficulties facing policy consistency and the identification of common interests, and the issue of burden-sharing across a wide range of areas and institutional contexts. The discussion in this chapter has important implications for these key elements of change, and it also reflects the fact that the US and the EC are central players in the processes of transformation. There is an intimate link between what have previously been regarded as 'domestic' debates and the question of international order, both at the global and at the European level.

The first sense in which this linkage can be identified is simply expressed: the US and the EC are central to each other, by virtue of the interdependence between their economies, political systems and societies. At the level of market interdependence, the continuing growth of flows of goods, capital, ideas and people means that the US and the EC are vital players in each other's 'domestic' arenas. In this respect, they reflect the growth of global structures of production and exchange, but they are also more intensely and broadly connected than any other major players in the global system. This market interdependence, however, does not exist in a political and security vacuum: the essential backcloth to the growth of economic interpenetration has been the constant yet constantly changing mutual involvement of Americans and Europeans in the alliance and associated structures. Security interdependence between the USA, the EC and other actors means that each is part of the security debate and redefinition which we have noted here. Finally, it is clear that market interdependence and security interdependence have gone alongside an intense and growing policy interdependence between the Atlantic partners. Actions taken on what appears to be a purely 'domestic' level have inevitable spillover effects in the 'domestic' arena of the other partner, and the planning of policy initiatives or responses must take into account this intimate set of linkages.

It is not sufficient, though, simply to draw attention to the fact that the US and the EC are intimately interconnected. The second feature of the coexistence and mutual entanglement between the two entities is their centrality to the European and world order. Such centrality has been the case since the inception of the relationship, but the trends noted in Chapter 1 have given it a new significance in the 1990s. In the United States, the debate about the 'New World Order' and the American role within it has taken a paradoxical course. On the one hand, the triumphalism of those who see the USA as the only superpower has been tempered by those who see it as the lonely superpower; the tension between assertive internationalism, selective engagement and neo-isolationism has been a constant theme of the debate since the collapse of the Soviet bloc. At the same time, the combination of perceived political primacy and economic vulnerability has given the debate another twist, with the resultant uncertainty about Washington's commitment to the multilateral trading and financial system. American policy has displayed considerable ambivalence about the interests to be pursued, and about the ability of US policies to determine events; after all, the leverage available through cold-war weapons and institutions, or through the industrial and economic ascendancy of the US economy, is now no longer to be taken for granted. In both cases, the spillover of American concerns into the world arena brings them into contact with the Europeans and, more particularly, the Community. Perceptions of economic vulnerability have fed on the development of the SEM programme and on the problems of achieving agreement in the Uruguay Round, where the EC is the chief actor, while the transformation of the European security context has provoked debate about the appropriate role for both the USA and the Community after the cold war.[20]

As for the Community itself, the debates about EMU and EPU, and the aftermath of the Maastricht agreements, have highlighted some enduring features of the Community's international role. On the one hand, the combination of the SEM programme, the debate on EPU and the continuing stalemate in the Uruguay Round have raised questions about the type of 'Europe' represented by the EC. While it has gained in weight and magnetism, it has not left behind the internal tensions between an 'open' and 'closed' economic stance. The ambivalence of Community responses to the approaches of others in Europe, from the EFTA countries through the east Europeans to the former Soviet republics, serves to underline this tension – a tension in which the USA is also implicated, both by history and by concrete involvement and interests. Alongside this well-established area of policy dilemmas there is now the much broader issue of political and security order. For a Community which has found it difficult to decide the balance of benefits between a continuing role as 'civilian power' and the increasing assertion of its distinctive security priorities, the 1990s pose fundamental challenges. As in the American case, it is impossible to disentangle the internal Community debate about political union from the changing security context in Europe, if for no other reason than that the Germans will not allow the two to become detached. Once this connection is made, then the link to the United States via the alliance is automatic, as is the emergence of the Community as a factor in the US domestic debate about security and world order. Once again, the EC and the USA are part of each other's internal make-up and debate, and essential elements in each other's policymaking processes.[21]

Conclusion

It has been argued here that both the USA and the Community have been engaged in a process of self-redefinition during the past two decades, but especially during the past five years: the United States in the aftermath of the 'high Reaganite' era and the ending of the cold war, the Community in the wake of the SEM programme and the transformation of Europe. In neither case is the process complete, and in neither case is it free of internal contradictions with major policy implications. Both the United States and the Community have difficulties of a 'domestic' nature concerning their internal structures and the demands of important policy constituencies, which have stimulated vigorous debates about the forms and functions of governance. At the same time, both are in the process of re-examining or redefining their policymaking processes, and the re-examinations have both procedural and substantive implications. Finally, the United States and the Community are both confronted with important questions about their present and future international orientations and roles. Although these take different forms and pose apparently different challenges, they place both the Community and the United States at the centre of international developments for the remainder of the 1990s. The issue for debate, in the light of the arguments made here, is whether there is the basis for an expansion of effective collaboration between the Americans and the Europeans, and what forms such collaboration might usefully take. Closely linked to this question is that of the 'models' provided by the United States and the Community, and the ways in which they might be relevant to the needs and aspirations of emerging political systems both in Europe and elsewhere. From this it can be seen that the changing identities of the transatlantic partners are a matter of crucial concern to the world as a whole. The following chapters will explore the issues in greater detail, focusing first on the changing economic order and then on the political order.

3

CHANGING ROLES IN THE WORLD ECONOMY

Chapters 1 and 2 have drawn attention to two central conditioning factors in the roles of the United States and the European Community in the world economy. First, there is the impact of radical structural change accompanied by the growth of interdependence and interpenetration. Second, there is the presence in both the EC and the USA of domestic doubt and debate about the governing of economic activities. The two factors are linked, and this is the basis of some of the greatest policy dilemmas facing governing authorities on both sides of the Atlantic. This chapter considers the changing roles of the EC and the US in the international economy, and the ways in which these intersect to shape the context for Euro-Atlantic relations. In so doing, it considers not only empirical changes in the positions occupied by the two entities, but also changes in the ways in which their respective roles are perceived and expressed. As noted in Chapter 1, change affecting the roles of each entity, and thus the 'Euro-Atlantic' relationship, has been spread over a number of decades. The current focus on the need for a redefinition of the relationship therefore results as much from a cognitive change among policy elites as from objective trends. This is particularly the case for macroeconomic and trade relations, where a progressive reduction in US willingness to sustain the multilateral system and provide leadership in the management of the world economy has been taking place for two decades or more.

The chapter focuses on four main areas of discussion:

(1) It explores the ways in which the EC's economic weight has grown relative to that of the US, and the ways in which this has shaped their

mutual perceptions. In addition, it explores the ways in which the shifting EC/US balance relates to the broader growth of economic interdependence and interpenetration, and the implications this has for broad directions of policy.

(2) It assesses systemic differences between the EC and the US and the ways in which these have become more obvious in the post-cold-war period. These systemic differences, together with differences in the decisionmaking capabilities and procedures of the USA and the Community, are likely to mean that EC and US approaches to problems arising from the increasing degree of international economic interdependence will be significantly different, and that issues of internal governance will increasingly form part of the agenda for Euro-Atlantic economic relations.

(3) It explores the evidence for the growth of economic blocs, centred in this case on the USA and the Community and expressing either an expansive or a defensive form of regionalism within the world economy. In particular, the chapter assesses the extent to which the growth of formal or informal economic blocs poses a threat to the multilateral system around which US/EC relations have centred for much of their existence.

(4) Finally, it analyses problems of policy coordination, first at the level of government in the USA and the Community, and then in the context of calls for increasing international coordination, both in the trade and in the macroeconomic field. There is evidence that both the United States and the EC have distinctive problems in this area, and that this will have a formative influence on their relations in the broader context of the world economy.

Relative economic weight

Compared with the dramatic political changes of the period 1989–91, and the subsequent crises in Europe and elsewhere, the changes in the international economy have assumed a much less sensational form. There has been no event in the international economy equivalent to the collapse of the Berlin Wall or the disintegration of the USSR, although both have had important economic implications. But this does not mean that economic changes have not been important. Major changes are taking place in the structure and functioning of the international economy and the respective roles of the EC and the US. Not only this, but perceptions of change, and of its economic and political implications, can also occur much more quickly than real changes in the international economy.

A fundamental change in the world economy is the growing weight of the EC. It has a GDP of $5.5 trillion (1990), only slightly smaller than the USA's $6 trillion. Extra-EC trade accounts for no less than 16% of total world exports. The degree to which the EC is internalizing multi-lateralism is, however, reflected in the fact that it accounts for 41% of world exports if one includes intra-EC trade (up from 36% in 1980). The EC member states account for 41% (1990) of US foreign direct investment (FDI), up from 34% in 1984 – in part as a result of the dynamism generated by the programme of the single European market (SEM). EFTA plus the EC, i.e. the European Economic Area (EEA) accounts for 47% of US FDI. Relatively stable economic growth during the 1980s has meant that the EC has become one of the most prosperous areas of the world, more or less on a par with the United States and Japan. This shapes external perceptions of the Community, even though the situation seen from within the EC often looks very different. Income and prosperity is not particularly evenly distributed throughout the EC, and 1991 and 1992 have been years of economic slowdown or recession. But for Americans the EC is no longer viewed as economically weak and in need of support as a bulwark against communism. For its neighbours to the east and south, the Community is seen as a zone of prosperity and stability, while even the Community's richer neighbours in EFTA regard it as the core of the European economy.

The SEM programme, and moves to create a monetary union in the second half of the 1980s, did much to shape these perceptions of the EC. At the end of the 1970s, the European Community was seen to have lost momentum. In the late 1970s and early 1980s there was a view, espe-cially in business and official circles in the United States, that the European economies were being held back by rigidities in capital and labour markets. Structural adjustment and deregulation was urged upon European governments in order to stimulate their economies. 'Euro-sclerosis' was the catchword of the period. The second half of the 1980s brought about a major change. Indeed for a period perceptions of 'Eurosclerosis' were replaced by 'Europhoria'. Much of this change was brought about by changes in national policies, such as the shift away from interventionist industrial policies in France in 1983 and the general move towards more deregulation led by Conservative governments in Britain.

These national policies were then overlaid with the EC's single market programme, which was itself seen by European business and many politicians as a response to Eurosclerosis. The SEM programme helped create a new dynamism, which caused the EC to be viewed now as being at 'the cutting edge' of international change.[1] Economic growth clearly provided a positive environment for the policy- and market-led integration which, from 1987 onwards, made the creation of a genuine internal market seem credible. The slowing of economic growth, or indeed the economic downturn, in 1991 and 1992 has tempered the pace of integration and led to doubts about whether the objectives set by the Community will be achieved.

Community competence is also being extended to more and more policies of relevance to international commerce. One of the main factors in this process has been a correlation between the growth of Community competence and the degree of interpenetration of national economies. The EC therefore not only has more weight; it brings this weight to bear in more and more areas of policy. For example, the Treaty of Rome (and Paris) from the outset provided significant Community competence covering tariff and non-tariff barriers, which has been augmented through the introduction of secondary legislation. The SEM programme in particular has extended Community competence into areas such as non-tariff barriers in the shape of different national regulatory policies. This has meant that as commercial policy has spread to encompass non-tariff barriers and regulatory barriers, the Community's single voice has also been extended. The broad impact of structural change in the world trading system has thus fed the growing weight and salience of the Community itself.

The Maastricht Treaty on European Union, if ratified, will also take the competence of the Community into further areas by providing qualified majority voting in the field of environmental policy, which is at the same time one of the new issues on the international commercial policy agenda for the 1990s. In the field of competition policy and its interaction with trade policy and market access, another 'new agenda' item, the EC already has extensive competence as a result of Articles 85 and 86 and 90–93 of the Treaty of Rome and the merger control regulation adopted in 1989.

Just as tariff barriers have given way to non-tariff barriers, regulatory barriers and structural impediments in international commercial policy, trade has given way to investment as the main channel of exchange. Here also the EC is progressively extending its competence. In the Uruguay Round of trade negotiations, it has negotiated for the twelve member states on the investment and services issues, just as on trade in goods. Likewise, in the OECD negotiations on investment, the Commission has assumed a role similar to its role as sole negotiator in the GATT, although some member states were reluctant to grant it this increased influence.

The most significant extension of Community competence of all, however, would be the creation of a single currency and thus a single voice in monetary and exchange-rate policies, if or when the Maastricht treaty is ratified. In contrast to its strength in trade policy, the EC has never had a single voice in monetary and exchange-rate policy. This has not been for want of trying. There was an early attempt to create economic and monetary union in the form of the Werner Plan in 1969, but this failed in the face of the pressures created by the floating of exchange rates after the decision to end the dollar standard. In the early 1970s, European currencies were relatively more exposed to external shocks, such as the oil crisis and exchange-rate fluctuations, than the US. This provided the motivation for numerous attempts to help stabilize exchange rates, often implicitly or explicitly as a response to American policies. First came the Werner Plan, adopted in 1971 with its associated proposals for the so-called currency snake. This failed in the face of pressures caused *inter alia* by the 1973 oil crisis. It was followed by the European Monetary System, introduced in 1979 as the result of a Franco-German initiative. The success of the EMS in stabilizing European exchange rates and helping to bring about a convergence of rates of inflation provided the basis for another effort to create EMU, which started in July 1988 at the Hanover meeting of the European Council.[2]

The agreement on EMU was the most significant element of the Maastricht agreement, but even so there are clearly grave doubts about whether EMU and a single currency will be established, as envisaged, by 1999 at the latest. First, doubt stems from whether Maastricht will be ratified at all, given that the British parliament and the Danish electorate still have to give their approval. Even if it is ratified there are still doubts about whether countries will be judged, by the European Council, to have met the convergence criteria set down on the size of public debt (60% of GDP), budget deficits (3% of GDP) and inflation (average no more than 1.5% above the average of the three EC member states having the lowest rate of inflation). If they are to meet these criteria, some member states, such as Italy and Belgium, will have to bring about structural changes to their economies in order to reduce public debt. Even Germany will have to take tough action to rein in public spending caused by unification if it is to meet the 3% fiscal deficit criterion.

Collectively these measures would have a deflationary effect on the EC, at least in the short term.[3] Coming at a time of general economic slowdown or outright recession, such deflationary prospects are highly unwelcome: some governments may not be able to contain the pressure to realign exchange rates within the exchange-rate mechanism (ERM) in order to mitigate the effects of discipline imposed by the German monetary authorities, itself aimed at controlling German inflation of more than 4%. While realignment is possible during stage one of EMU, which the EC entered into in July 1990, such a development would raise doubts about the determination of countries to meet the convergence criteria. As the SEM programme showed, credibility is a vital element of success in European integration.

Despite the uncertainties of ratification and the economic pressures, the odds are that some member states will achieve EMU before the end of the decade. It this does indeed prove to be the case, what impact would it have on the EC's role in the world? EMU would increase the weight of the EC, but any such increase will be progressive. Germany already has considerable weight by itself and this would be augmented by EMU. The ECU is not about to replace the dollar as the main reserve currency overnight, and much trade, particularly in sensitive commodities such as oil, will continue to be denominated in dollars. But the role of the ECU could increase more rapidly if EC policies were, as promised by Maastricht, geared to price stability, and if US policies became relatively more flexible. In this event, funds would flow into the ECU, especially at times of uncertainty. Even without a single currency the role of the European currencies and authorities, and in particular the Deutschmark and the Bundesbank, will increase.

Finally, the weight of the Community is being enhanced by the magnetic effect it is having on its neighbours. On 22 October 1991 the EC concluded the European Economic Area negotiations with the EFTA countries; in so doing, it effectively extended the Community 'model' of market integration to the EFTA in most sectors, creating a common market of 380 million people. The areas excluded from the EEA are agriculture, transport and, of course, the more supranational elements of the EC. Jacques Delors originally conceived of the EEA as, at least in part, a means of heading off new applications for Community membership. In this respect it failed. Austria (July 1989), Sweden (July 1991), Finland (March 1992) and Switzerland (May 1992), as well as Malta and Turkey, have already applied for membership, and Norway may yet follow at the end of 1992.

This pending enlargement of the Community depends in part on the outcome of the Maastricht ratification process and an agreement on the financing of the EC according to the so-called 'Delors II' package. It also creates internal pressures with regard to the institutional structure of the EC, but none the less it means that the Community will continue to 'internalize' more and more of the multilateral process. More countries will accept the *acquis communautaire* (i.e. the established EC norms) and thus be effectively integrated into the EC's sphere of influence. This will occur even without full membership. Thus the Europe Agreements between the EC and the central and east European countries also extend the *acquis* in the sense that, in establishing the institutional structure of market economies, these countries are using EC legislation and regulations as a model. This does not constitute a conscious effort on the part of the EC to supplant multilateralism, but such 'expansive regionalism'[4] has a similar effect. As in the case of the SEM programme and EMU, the enlargement will therefore result in a largely unintended enhancement of the EC's role in the international economy.

At the same time as perceptions of the EC's economic weight and influence have shifted, there has been a relative decline in the weight and influence of the United States. As set out in Chapter 2, this is felt mainly as regards America's competitive position. For some years there has been a growing concern about the ability of the US to compete in international markets. Above all, Japanese industrial competition is seen as 'hollowing out' American industry. The renewed dynamism of Europe in the period from 1988 to 1991 added to this sense of America slipping behind in the competitive race.

One of the results was a revival of the debate about structural weaknesses within the United States such as the collapse of infrastructure and the inadequacies in US education, especially vocational education programmes. It is normal for such arguments to be made in the run-up to presidential elections. Indeed the Democratic Party made very similar arguments during 1987. But four years later concern about such structural weaknesses was more widespread. Business representatives shared many of the concerns because of the growing problems of finding a well-trained and educated workforce. Even committed internationalists were prepared to argue that domestic weaknesses were undermining the ability of the United States to play an active role in international affairs. In other words, concern about domestic industrial performance had become more general. It was no longer the case that it was only protectionist, inward-looking lobbies that were concerned with it. This had an overall impact on US policy towards trade and commercial policy. In 1987 Senator Gephardt's proposals on reciprocity were seen to be on the protectionist side of the debate leading up to the 1988 Omnibus Trade and Competitiveness Act, but by 1991 similar proposals were more or less in the mainstream of Congressional and interest-group thinking.

It must be stressed that what is involved is a relative decline in the economic weight of the United States. It remains one of the richest societies and the single largest economy in the world, and it is open to dispute how far the predominance of the period 1945–80 was a freak occurrence in a relatively stable longer-term picture. As a result, US policymakers have considerable economic leverage at their disposal. The threat of closing the US market represents a potent policy instrument and one which the US administration has been able to deploy with some effect in its application of Section 301 actions against countries which the US feels are using unfair trade practices or policies. The fact that, more and more frequently, the US is considering recourse to such unilateral policy instruments reflects, however, a loss of confidence in its ability to influence and shape the nature of the international system. This is particularly the case vis-à-vis the EC, which by virtue of the size of its market and its importance for the US is able to challenge US policy in virtually any area of commercial activity.

How does this perception of the USA's changing status and role intersect with American perceptions of the Community? In the USA, there has been a tendency for perceptions of the EC to move in cycles: thus in the late 1970s the Community was seen as irrelevant by many in Washington, but by the late 1980s the same policymakers and political or business leaders were prone to see a 'united states of Europe' as lying just over the horizon. Although in the early 1990s there has been a swing back to the view that the Community has lost momentum and has turned inwards, this has occurred in circumstances of intensifying market integration and has been conditioned by perceptions of the EC's growing weight. Thus an introspective or defensive EC means more to the USA now than it did in the late 1970s or even the mid-1980s. As will be seen in Chapter 4, the changing political status of the Community adds a new dimension to this set of perceptions.

Systemic differences
Chapter 2 indicated that systemic differences exist between the US and the EC. Whereas the predominant model of the market economy in the European Community is the *social market economy*, the prevailing US model is the *free market economy*. In part, these differences are

reflections of the empirical structures and performance of the respective economies, but they also reflect ideological distinctions which gain expression in political debate.

The European social market economy consists of various elements. There is a safety net in the shape of extensive social policies, such as unemployment benefits, national health care systems and social security schemes. These all result in higher public spending on social programmes in Europe and thus a higher proportion of GDP going on taxes (about 35% compared with 22% in the US). There is also a desire to retain a social consensus. In many continental European countries social consensus is seen as a precondition for economic prosperity. It is designed to ensure that all economic actors, the 'social partners' (i.e. labour and capital), identify themselves with longer-term objectives of stable economic growth and prosperity. In free market systems, such as the US during the 1980s, social programmes are seen as at best a necessary evil, and in all cases as a cost burden on competitiveness and the attainment of long-term economic prosperity. In free market economies, there is an emphasis on releasing the forces of enterprise, the benefits of which trickle down to the rest of society. Although the presidential platforms of 1992 reveal significant differences between Democrat and Republican views of this process, the framework for debate is essentially unshaken.

The EC itself is heterogenous, with distinct variations between the extensive social market provision of countries such as Germany or Denmark and the relatively free market structures of the United Kingdom. But there are also quite strong pressures to extend the concepts of the social market economy at the Community level, which attract varying coalitions of supporters and opponents. There are policies to promote economic *cohesion*, i.e. (modest) redistribution of resources among EC member states. There is also the *social dimension* to European integration: the attempt to reach an EC-wide agreement on the level of social provisions, and active efforts to promote a *social dialogue* between labour and employers at an EC level.[5]

There is also a stronger tradition of an active state in Europe than in the US – a tradition which has survived the liberalization of the 1980s and of the SEM programme. The state is still seen to have a legitimate and leading role in the provision of education, R&D and infrastructure.[6] Alongside this tendency, there are also the remnants of national industrial policies and the beginnings of EC industrial policies in sectors such as electronics and, to a lesser degree, cars.[7] The Maastricht agreement included a chapter on industrial policy (Article 130 EU), although it is unclear how much effect this will have even if the treaty is ratified, since it will still require unanimity. The structural weaknesses in the US have led to a revival of the US debate about industrial policy, but as in the past this has to contend with an established bias against an active role for the state in industrial affairs, at least outside the defence industries.[8]

The liberalization measures of the SEM programme have also not yet effected a complete denial of national industrial identity; indeed, in many countries, there remains a close identification between state authorities and indigenous companies or industries. This means that while explicit, statutory national champion policies are no longer viable because of EC controls and market considerations, some countries continue to promote their indigenous industries. There is a distinction between national champion policies, in which the national market is kept as exclusive preserve for the national company, and the promotion of international champions, in which competition exists on the companies' home market, but the government still provides support. The form of ownership of companies also means that it is still possible, despite the SEM programme, for companies to retain their national character and ownership. In short, with the limited exception of the UK, there is no open market for corporate control in the member states of the EC, as there is in the United States, where the large, open capital market contributes to a relatively weak identification with 'national' companies.[9]

These differences inevitably mean that there is an element of competition between the two models or systems which affects trade and economic relations. This has existed for some time and has, for example, shaped the respective EC and US approaches to efforts to develop harmonized rules in the GATT. The end of the cold war has removed the overriding security imperative to cooperate which helped to contain such trade competition. Even during the late 1970s and the onset of the so-called 'new cold war', the Tokyo Round of trade negotiations was concluded at a time of considerable transatlantic tension over the 'twin-track' decision to deploy intermediate nuclear forces in western Europe. There was no direct linkage between the issues, but the desire to avoid exacerbating frictions within the alliance provided a strong incentive to reach agreement on trade disputes. There is no equivalent incentive in the case of the Uruguay Round, and as a result the influence of domestic factors and systemic competition has been particularly apparent.

The demise of Soviet communism may also have moved the ideological goalposts. As long as it was assumed that the dominant axis of competition was that between capitalism and communism it was easier to overlook differences between the types of capitalism.[10] The collapse of the USSR and the 'triumph' of market economics means that there is a greater awareness of what are material differences between the American, European and Japanese models of the market economy. As already noted, there is of course no one single model of capitalism in Europe. Indeed one of the characteristics of the European model is that it encompasses quite different forms, such as the 'Anglo-Saxon' and 'Rheinland' models.[11] The Italian model differs yet again, with its public enterprise and relatively closed capital market. France has adopted the market-based elements of the Anglo-Saxon model, while striving for the consistency and long-term orientation of Rheinland capitalism.

This heterogeneity within Europe has influenced European thinking on how to deal with economic integration, and has contributed to a divergence between European and US approaches to commercial policy. The European experience has taught that harmonization is not a viable approach. Differences between national approaches are such that resistance to harmonization was in no small measure responsible for the 'sclerosis' in the EC policymaking process of the late 1970s and early 1980s. The EC's 'new approach', reflected in the Single European Act and SEM programme, sought to minimize harmonization and ensure, through mutual recognition, that national or systemic differences were accommodated and not used as the pretext for protectionism. Without this experience, the USA still tends to see agreement on a (harmonized) set of multilateral rules as the natural and desirable approach. Understandably, there is also a tendency to see the US system as the most appropriate basis for such rules. Meanwhile, the relative decline in US influence means it is less able to ensure that US-framed rules will prevail over EC or Japanese variants. The danger in this situation is that when US objectives are (inevitably) frustrated, there is domestic pressure to revert to unilateral approaches in which the US effectively seeks to impose its understanding of 'fair trade' on its trading partners.

Multilateralism versus regional blocs
The European Community
The rejuvenation of the EC during the second half of the 1980s has had important implications for multilateralism, in two ways. First, by the extension of its membership and competence the EC is effectively internalizing parts of the multilateral process. Whereas in the past there were eighteen European countries, there is now effectively a single *acquis*

communautaire, which is followed by the twelve as well as by six EFTA countries. As noted above, this situation applies in more and more areas of commercial policy. In order to remove barriers to trade within the EC and to complete the internal market, the Community has developed an extensive array of policy instruments from competition policy, through standards and policies on national subsidies, to liberalization measures for services such as financial services and telecommunications. Policies in these fields draw on experience in other countries, such as the United States, or on policies and procedures in multilateral bodies such as the GATT or OECD, but the EC effectively devises its own approach. As discussed above, this is often different from the US approach. These differences therefore define a distinct regional bloc in the sense that the European approach differs from the US or the Japanese. There are, in other words, competing regulatory spheres of influence.[12]

The efforts to create a genuine internal market therefore have implications for the multilateral system because the solutions that the Community finds to its internal barriers or problems tend to pre-empt at least some of the multilateral debate on the topic. For example, the EC has developed a regime for dealing with national public purchasing, which influenced the Community's position on GATT negotiations on the same topic. Likewise, the established principles of EC competition policy or environmental policy will influence any multilateral negotiations on those topics.

The Community also shapes the multilateral process by decisions it takes in bilateral and multilateral negotiations. Unlike the North American Free Trade Area (NAFTA), the EC has a common commercial policy. It therefore has one voice in important trade negotiations. During the course of the multilateral round of GATT talks which began in September 1986, the EC was repeatedly accused of being preoccupied with internal developments. This was particularly the case at the end of 1990 when the Community moved to initiate the two intergovernmental conferences (IGCs) on economic and monetary union and political union but was unable to reach a common negotiating position on agriculture in the Uruguay Round. The failure of the EC to agree on a common position was seen, by other member states, as the main reason for the failure of the GATT negotiations in Brussels in December 1990.

There is some evidence to support the case that the EC was preoccupied during 1990. There was a full agenda for the Community, as for others, at the end of the 1980s and the beginning of the 1990s: at one level this included the SEM programme, the two IGCs and thus the future shape of the European Union, and the related negotiations on the EEA and possible enlargement. Alongside this, though, the Community had to deal with German unification and the related question of its policy towards the eastern and central part of the continent, relations with the USSR and then the CIS, not to mention the Gulf war and the Yugoslav crisis. In these circumstances it is understandable that ministers and officials had limited time to devote to the GATT negotiations. A further factor was that the negotiations were so complex. This made it difficult for politicians and business groups to get involved. European business has, in any case, adopted a different – less hands-on – approach to multilateral negotiations than American business. Having made their positions clear, European business lobbies tend to leave the negotiations to the negotiators. The negotiators themselves, namely the Commission and the responsible national officials, were, like their US counterparts, committed to completing the multilateral negotiations, but the context within which they approached the task differed in important respects from that to be found on the other side of the Atlantic.

Another way of looking at the role of the EC in the international economy, and thus at its credentials as a regional bloc, is to ask whether the Community represents an effective *process* for dealing with economic interdependence rather than developing the capacity to operate effectively as *an actor* in its own right. The EC as a process has been enhanced by the Single European Act (SEA), with its qualified majority voting provisions and the 'new approach' of the EC moving towards more mutual recognition and away from harmonizing everything. Broadly speaking, the EC as a process has succeeded by removing the ability of national governments to limit trade or investment within the EC. In only a few cases has it resulted in these powers being replaced by central powers in the hands of the Community.[13] The SEM programme worked because national governments recognized the need to limit their own powers, but this does not mean that they are prepared to cede new powers to the centre.

This tendency can also be observed in the EMU debate. In order to create a single currency the monetary sovereignty of the member states must be removed, but there is no agreement on granting discretionary power over monetary policy to the EC. In the case of monetary policy, the approach is to have an independent European Central Bank (ECB). In other words the *relative* weakness of the central policymaking functions in the EC could well be extended to the monetary policy area.

The reluctance to cede discretionary powers to a central political authority means that the EC will tend to be more effective as a process than as a discrete actor. It is important to put this into context. The Community clearly does have some decisionmaking capabilities and it does reach agreed positions on trade and commercial policy issues, albeit with some difficulty. But it does not have, and will not have for some considerable time, if ever, central powers equivalent to those of the US. This raises the question of how the Community can ensure that decisions implementing commercial policy measures, or in the future monetary and exchange rate policies, form part of a coherent foreign economic policy. During the intergovernmental negotiations, the Commission proposed that there should be a coherent approach to all external actions of the Community, including trade, money, aid and foreign policy, but this was rejected because it would result in too much centralization. There is an awareness of the issues at stake. For example, in the early months of 1990 many political leaders called for political union precisely so that the Community could respond effectively to the challenges of dealing with changes in east and central Europe and the responsibilities likely to fall to the EC as a result. The Maastricht agreement provides the basis for a CFSP, which could be used to develop a coherent foreign economic policy, but this remains speculative at present.

The North American 'bloc'

When considering the credentials of the so-called regional bloc in the Americas, there are important distinctions to be drawn with the Community. The North American regional trading organizations, such as the NAFTA, do not internalize the multilateral process in the same way as the EC. With no common commercial policy and only rudimentary common institutions, in the shape of dispute settlement arrangements, the 'North American bloc' is very different from the EC, which has a common commercial policy, a distinct supranational legal order and aspirations of monetary and political union. In terms of the global economy, it therefore may be more appropriate to view the USA itself as 'the bloc'.

It is important here to consider what constitutes a 'bloc'. In the current usage it appears to have three characteristics. First, it must have economic muscle. The US clearly qualifies here: despite some relative decline, it is still a major force in international commercial relations. Adding Mexico and Canada means that NAFTA becomes larger than even an enlarged EC in terms of population, but the absence of a common commercial policy means it cannot put this collective economic muscle to use.

Second, a bloc is generally seen as an area in which the interests of the constituent states take precedence over those outside. If one sees the US federal government as representing the diverse interests of individual US states in international negotiations, then the US qualifies also in this sense. US commercial policies are shaped by a balance of interests among the US states, i.e. between the farming states and those in which there is a concentration of high technology or service industries. US macroeconomic policy also seeks to balance the interests of the various states. For example, the vast majority of jobs lost during the recession of 1990–91 were lost in the northeastern seaboard states, so that the pressure for expansion came most strongly from those states, while California was pressing less hard for expansionary policies. In addition, increased international economic integration and interpenetration of national economies mean that actions of the individual states can limit market access or promote inward investment.

Given the reluctance of the Congress to legislate for the states, the individual US states can thus shape US commercial policy. This means that federal policy is, to a greater or lesser degree, determined by what the states will allow the federal government to do, or more accurately by whatever understanding is reached between the state and federal levels. In this sense, therefore, internal deals shape US policy in a similar fashion to the ways in which they shape EC policy and can mean that the domestic interests prevail over those of the USA's trading partners. This has happened with regard to various issues in the Uruguay Round, such as the regulation of financial services. The states have also frustrated more 'enlightened' policies of the federal government in the field of public purchasing or investment. An enlightened policy here means one devised to promote US interests in the multilateral system. Thus on public purchasing the US wanted better access for US exporters. Given the strength of its negotiating partners, this could be achieved only by offering enhanced access to the US market. State purchasing and purchasing polices determine access to 70% of the public sector contracts in the US.

Third, for a 'bloc' to exist it has to have a discrete identity, a difference which sets it apart from the rest. The US has this by virtue of the fact that it has federal powers and that US trade legislation seeks to determine what is 'fair trade'. In other words, the US has a clear, distinct view of what rules should shape international economic relations. In this context, NAFTA is important as an expression of some kind of 'regional' identity, but what were the main motivations of the participating countries? Its origins go back to the US/Canada auto agreement in the 1960s. At about the time the Uruguay Round of multilateral negotiations was launched (1986), the US and Canada began bilateral trade negotiations. For the US, one of the objectives was to show the rest of the world how trade agreements could be negotiated and thus set a precedent for the GATT round. There was also a desire to enhance access for US goods, services and investment. For Canada, which conducts 70% of its trade with the US, the motive was similar to that of the EFTA countries in Europe: namely, to 'get inside' US trade remedy laws and ensure that it would not suffer if the US shifted to a more protectionist policy.

The US/Canada Free Trade Agreement was concluded in early 1988 and was finally ratified after the Canadian elections later that year. In the event, it was a more modest agreement than originally envisaged. Tariffs are to be reduced over a period of ten years from the coming into force of the agreement on 1 January 1989, and some non-tariff barriers will be reduced. In important areas such as services, public procurement and technical standards the agreement went further than existing multilateral agreements, but did not, as many in the US and elsewhere had hoped, provide a model for the more ambitious Uruguay Round, except on negotiating techniques. In many areas, such as services, the US/Canada FTA was essentially a stand-still on new restrictions. It also proved impossible to agree on common rules where systemic differences were more pronounced, such as on the use of subsidies.

A central issue in the FTA was dispute settlement. Canada, which had long complained of procedural protectionism by the US through the use of trade remedies such as countervailing duty and anti-dumping duties, wanted to ensure that these were disciplined by the agreement. The US Congress was reluctant to cede sovereignty to an extranational disputes procedure, but a compromise was found which provides for a three-stage procedure. Efforts are first made to reach a negotiated agreement; if this fails there are two options: binding arbitration (if both sides agree) or a panel of independent experts. The approach finally agreed is remarkable in the sense that it does begin to challenge the absolute sovereignty of US trade remedy legislation.

In contrast to the EC, in which rulings of the European Court of Justice are binding on national governments, the FTA contains little in the shape of supranational powers and, as noted above, no common external commercial policy. The US and Canada thus retain the freedom to pursue their own trade and investment policies. Nor is there any obligation to accept harmonization of domestic policies or anything equivalent to the EC's mutual recognition and home country control provisions to promote convergence. As in the EC, there are strong market-led pressures, so that a form of *de facto* competition between the US and Canadian rules certainly exists. But there is no policy integration to back this up.

In early 1990 the initiative was taken to extend the free trade agreement to include Mexico in a North American Free Trade Agreement. Mexico, like Canada before it, had a clear interest in consolidating market access and 'getting inside' US trade remedy laws, thus pre-empting any possible shift towards a more protectionist policy in the US. The Mexican interest was also motivated by fear that the US and other OECD countries were becoming preoccupied with central and eastern Europe and the Soviet Union. But neither Mexico nor Canada seek closer integration in a regional bloc which would be dominated by the USA.

The Bush administration was initially cool on the NAFTA idea, out of a concern that such negotiations might jeopardize the GATT negotiations. After a few months, however, it supported the initiative, not as a means of creating a trade bloc to compete with the EC, but more to help consolidate economic reform in Mexico. This would in turn benefit US exporters and help contain the flow of migrants into the US. As with the FTA, there was opposition from Congress and from organized labour. Congress was not prepared to cede sovereign control over trade remedies; and, for its part, organized labour, supported by Democrats in Congress, wished to influence Mexican social legislation to prevent 'social dumping' and ensure US firms could not evade environmental controls north of the Rio Grande. The outline NAFTA agreement reached in July 1992 left many of these issues unresolved.

In June 1990 President Bush launched the Enterprise for the Americas Initiative (EAI) to establish a free trade and market economy zone 'from Anchorage to Terra del Fuego'. The EAI has three objectives: to promote free trade and open markets; to promote investment in South and Central America; and to find ways of easing the debt burden for the still heavily indebted countries. The basic motivation was more political than economic in that the objective was to consolidate the trend towards market liberalization and political reforms in Latin America. In this sense it could be seen as part of the effort to establish the 'new world order' sought by the Bush administration in the Americas. The desire to promote economic stability in neighbouring countries is similar to the European policy vis-à-vis central and eastern Europe and North Africa, and represents a shift away from the preoccupation with security interests in central America which characterized the Reagan years.

The NAFTA and the EAI could provide the foundations for a trade and currency bloc, but the US has gone out of its way to stress that any initiatives taken in 'the hemisphere' should not detract from multilateralism. Nor is the US seeking to pursue exclusive policies. At the Houston summit in June 1990, it offered the Europeans and Japanese an opportunity to participate by contributing to the investment fund arm of the EAI. Japan and Spain have since decided to support the fund, but Germany, Britain and Italy have not.

Neither the US nor the EC has actively sought to create regional blocs as alternatives to multilateralism. But the economic weight of each compared with most other trading entities means that they satisfy the size criterion for 'blocs'. In the case of the US this is so even without Canada and Mexico. In both cases much of the pressure for regional agreements has come from smaller neighbouring countries seeking guarantees against a protectionist drift in either US or EC policies. Both the EC and the US have distinctive approaches to commercial policy which reflect systemic differences. In this respect also, then, they satisfy the criteria for 'blocs', but the absence of a common commercial policy means that it is the US, rather than the NAFTA, which forms the 'bloc'.

In terms of what balance is struck between internal or domestic interests and multilateral responsibilities, one is not comparing like with like when one compares the EC and the US. The EC has gone much further towards policy integration and is therefore better placed to deal with the *process* of economic integration than the NAFTA. The need to reach agreement among the twelve means, however, that it has been less successful in articulating and carrying through a global trade strategy as part of Community foreign policy. If one accepts that the EC is more effective as a process, the question then becomes: how does the Community process mesh with the multilateral process? The NAFTA does not limit the ability of the US to initiate and articulate trade and foreign economic policies. Domestically, the interstate commerce clause of the US constitution grants the Congress powers to deal with virtually every aspect of (international) commercial policy, but there is political opposition from the individual states to some policies. Thus the question for US commercial policy is to what extent these pressures prevent it from fulfilling its responsibilities for the multilateral system.

The GATT Uruguay Round: a test of commitment to multilateralism
A key test of the respective roles of the US and the EC in the global economy is whether these internal preoccupations can be reconciled with multilateral responsibilities. Chapter 2 showed that both the United

States and the Community have domestic structural and political pre-occupations which could undermine their commitment to multilateralism. In both cases, there are strong sectoral interests to be overcome. In the EC, the agricultural lobbies have been strong enough to damage the EC's credibility in the Uruguay Round. In the US, the textile lobby very nearly did the same in the autumn of 1990. More broadly, there is a growing pressure for unilateralism in the US and a tendency to be preoccupied with European issues in the EC. At present, however, both the EC and the US continue to work for an effective multilateral trading system and take the GATT seriously.[14]

The US provided much of the momentum for the current Uruguay Round of trade talks. This grew out of Congress's desire, which has intensified during the course of the negotiations, to see other markets open. It has meant that the administration has had to set ambitious objectives in order to have a chance of persuading Congress to accept the final package. This has provided valuable momentum in the negotiations, but has also raised expectations, in terms of concrete improvements in market access, to a level that was never likely to be satisfied. The objective of creating stronger multilateral rules is still there, but, as the services negotiations have shown, an agreement which would provide the basis for future liberalization and prevent new measures that restrict trade is by itself not enough for the US. Such an agreement would have the effect of preventing the US from pursuing alternative unilateral or bilateral approaches to market liberalization without providing anything concrete in the way of multilateral liberalization. This is an outcome both business lobbies and Congress wish to avoid at all costs. The experience with unilateral approaches, such as the use or threat of action under Section 301 of the US trade legislation, has shown that using access to the US market as leverage can produce quicker results than multilateral approaches, so the last thing American domestic interests want is a multilateral discipline which prevents the remedial use of US trade legislation.

This determination to retain scope for unilateral action reflects a longer-term trend in the use of US trade legislation. From the early 1970s the US has sought to countervail or compensate for the effects of other countries' 'unfair trade' practices (read systemic differences). Thus the 1974 Trade Act strengthened domestic remedies in the shape of countervailing and anti-dumping actions, and introduced the broader Section 301 remedy for other forms of unfair trade. Initially the executive branch of government made full use of the discretionary power it was given under the legislation, and sought to balance domestic pressures and multilateral responsibilities rather than apply unilateral sanctions. Over the years Congress has become more and more frustrated with this reluctance to use these provisions, and subsequent legislation has progressively reduced the executive branch's discretion.

During the 1980s the emphasis of US policy thus shifted towards a more aggressive use of US trade legislation. This was reflected, for example, in the 1987 Gephardt amendment. The objective now is increasingly to change domestic practices of other countries where they are considered to be unfair – that is, where they do not correspond with the US idea of what policy and business practices should be. From a historical perspective this trend can be seen as follows. When the US was able to shape the multilateral system, during the 1950s and 1960s, there was little need for domestic remedies. During the 1970s, it became clear that the US could not push through multilateral rules which prohibited its trading partners pursuing different policies (such as subsidies) and there was a need to take countervailing action when these injured the affected US industries. In the 1980s, the perception grew that the GATT was not working; when this perception was combined with increased trade dependency, it was logical to conclude that the US also had to enhance the access for its exports and thus adopt more aggressive attempts to get errant trading partners to change their practices. 'Aggressive unilateralism' thus may seek to open markets, but it simultaneously undermines multilateralism because it pursues market opening on the basis of US law and US interpretations of what is 'fair trade'. This said, the threat of US unilateralism has none the less provided a (negative) incentive for the USA's trading partners to negotiate multilaterally, as indeed was the intention.

When the Uruguay Round entered what should have been its final phase in 1990, the US administration was not certain whether the package likely to emerge from the Brussels meeting of the GATT contacting parties in December 1990 would be sufficient to satisfy Congress. The administration could not risk accepting an agreement and then have Congress vote it down. The inflexible position of the EC on agriculture – the only real area in which it was the EC alone that was holding up agreement – therefore provided a way out of the dilemma for the US negotiators. By refusing to accept the modest EC concessions on agricultural liberalization, it was possible to have the round founder in Brussels, where the EC could take the blame. There was little incentive for the US to make concessions on agriculture. This, combined with the EC's domestic problems, such as the strength of the farming lobby and the political sensitivity of Franco-German relations, goes a long way to explain why the EC and the US failed to reach a compromise over agriculture.[15]

The expectations of the round in the EC were different from those in the United States, although, as in the US, there was a broad desire to see agreement on multilateral regimes. Initially the Community had been more sceptical about the round, but soon there developed a positive attitude. Unlike the US, however, the Community has not been faced with the kind of 'results or else' pressure which emanates from Congress or the business lobbies. The EC also has instruments, such as third country provisions in various directives (the Second Banking Coordination directive or the public purchasing directives, etc.) which could be used to pursue aggressive unilateralist policies, but there is no consensus among the member states on the use of such instruments. What some had intended should be the EC's equivalent of the Section 301 provisions in US trade law, the so-called New Commercial Policy Instrument agreed in 1985, was also watered down because of differences between member states, and cannot match the US provision in terms of potency. The relative absence of pressure for results and of any unilateralist instruments to defend meant that the EC was more prepared to accept GATT discipline over its third country provisions.

Another reason for the EC's willingness to see its instruments subject to GATT discipline was that it had a hidden agenda in the round. This was to ensure that US trade remedies such as Section 301 were subject to GATT discipline. In order to achieve this the EC had to accept multilateral discipline over its provisions. The important exception has been anti-dumping. Here the Commission and member states were pressured by industry to retain discretionary provisions. The bottom line for European industry was that without anything akin to Section 301 there was no effective means of defending itself against 'unfair' competition other than anti-dumping measures. In short, the EC has been less of a prime mover in the multilateral round, but at the same time it is not moving to a strategy of aggressive unilateralism. The nature of the Community and the absence of a consensus on trade policy help to explain both positions.

On most issues in the Uruguay Round, the EC was no more defensive than the US.[16] As noted, the one area on which it was isolated was agriculture. It is, however, a measure of its diplomatic failure in not adopting a more positive position on agriculture that the perception in the

53

US and many other countries is that it is protectionist. The agricultural interests, with their entrenched representation throughout the EC, and in particular in the Council of Agricultural Ministers, were able to hold the rest of the EC hostage. The inability to produce a sensible negotiating position in advance of the December 1990 Brussels meeting meant that the EC subsequently took the blame for the meeting's failure. Even after a further year of negotiation, it was again the EC which seemed most prepared to reject the draft final document submitted by Arthur Dunkel, the Secretary-General of the GATT, in December 1991. There is therefore a grave danger that the EC will further compound its diplomatic failure of December 1990, although there is considerable evidence that it will require an effort by both the Bush administration and the EC if there is to be an agreement outline before the November presidential election.

One important lesson from the GATT round is that the high degree of interpenetration of the US and EC economies makes it difficult for both sides to pursue coherent and consistent policies. In dealing with international security issues, such as the relationship between NATO and the EC or WEU, the constituencies involved are fairly small. In Washington parlance, they are 'within the Beltway', while in the EC they are largely contained in the foreign policy elites of the member states. For trade and investment, the constituencies are much wider and often beyond the control of the experts. In the US, the administration must always deal with two sets of negotiating partners, those in other countries and those in Congress. In the EC, trade policymaking is still relatively technocratic, but the need to reach agreement among the twelve creates inertia. This makes it hard for either the EC or the US to fulfil a leadership function in the multilateral system. On balance, the EC is more burdened by inertia, but it is also less likely to become aggressive in using its economic weight to get other countries to change their policies.

Nevertheless, both the EC and the US exercise a tremendous influence on the shape of the international trading system, probably too much influence. Smaller countries have a number of options. They can seek to strengthen the multilateral disciplines so as to contain the exercise of economic muscle by the EC and US. This is precisely what many are seeking to do in the Uruguay Round, and it helps to explain why many developing countries are more supportive of multilateral discipline than they were in the past. But the US (most-favoured-nation status in the General Agreement on Trade in Services), and to a lesser degree the EC (anti-dumping), resist efforts to bring their trade instruments under multilateral discipline.

For those countries neighbouring the EC or the US there may be the option of reaching free trade agreements with them, but not all countries have this option. An alternative is to try to increase your own muscle; the recently announced free trade area within ASEAN is perhaps a case in point. If none of these options are attractive or open to you, as is the case with Japan, the only thing left is to try to contain the protectionist pressures. Japan has done this by accommodating calls for bilateral agreements, but at the expense of giving credibility to the use of 'results-based' trade policies as a means of dealing with systemic differences between Japan on the one hand and the US and EC on the other.

Policy formulation

Higher levels of interpenetration, together with the linkage between economic and foreign and security policy issues, have added to the complexity of policy formulation and policy coordination. The respective roles of the EC and the US in the world economy will therefore depend, in part, on their ability to develop, articulate and carry through coherent foreign economic policies.

US views of the EC are affected by years of accumulated experience in trade negotiations. The prevailing view in the US administration at the beginning of the 1990s was that the Community, i.e. the Commission, would not negotiate seriously until it had obtained a mandate from the Council and could not negotiate thereafter because the mandate was so restrictive. This view owes much to the EC's behaviour on agriculture. It is not the case generally, since the Commission effectively negotiated on one mandate, set by the Council in the summer of 1986, throughout most of the Uruguay Round and still managed to make some major changes in position. But the fact that this perception exists is itself important.

The EC's problems over agriculture in the Uruguay Round illustrate how difficult it is for the Community to deliver a coherent policy line which places the wider Community interest over the interests of a specific party. If the Community is to be an active player in the international economy it must be able to do this. The fact that it cannot does not automatically mean that it is protectionist and inward-looking. The Community process can still have a liberalizing effect on markets, as is illustrated by much of the SEM programme. It simply means that it takes longer for the Community to come forward with concrete proposals.

In the light of the plans for EMU, the question arises as to the role of the EC in the field of international monetary and exchange-rate policy, and thus in international policy coordination in the G7 and other fora. If and when the EC moves to stage three of the Delors process and a single currency, the ECB will essentially decide on European monetary policy. Once a particular policy position has been adopted, it is unlikely to show much flexibility. The US is already used to the frustration of trying to get the Bundesbank to adopt a more flexible approach than one that always puts price stability first. If the ECB is to be based on the Bundesbank model, tensions between the EC and the US or other members of the G7 could become worse rather than better.

With a single currency the EC would also be more able to treat the external (i.e. extra-European) component of policy as a residual, in much the same way as the US was able to do until the 1980s. In the 1970s the Europeans were obliged to make sometimes painful domestic policy adjustments in order to defend their exchange rates. During the 1980s the European monetary system (EMS) remained vulnerable to changes in the value of the dollar and thus US domestic policy decisions, because unstable exchange rates threatened cohesion within the EMS. A decline in the dollar or low interest rates in the US could result in an inflow of funds into the D-mark and thus risk pushing it above its EMS limits. Within a single currency the participating countries would be less exposed to such external pressures.[17] The external dimension of policy decisions could therefore become less important.[18] In other words, there will be less pressure on the EC to act on monetary and exchange rates than in the past. This, combined with the difficulty of changing positions once agreed by the Twelve, could mean that the EC will also have little motivation and a limited ability to exercise a leadership function in international policy coordination. To use the same analogy as for trade, the EC could be more effective as a process – that of creating monetary stability in Europe – than as a player in international economic coordination. Again, the net effect need not be negative. It would, after all, be of benefit to the world as a whole to have a stable non-inflationary Europe. In an interdependent world economy much will depend on how the US perceives and responds to such a development.[19]

The prevailing US view of European monetary cooperation has been one of scepticism about its chances of success. This view influenced thinking about EMU when it was initially proposed in 1988, and it is a view which the results of the Danish and French referenda and the pressures on the ERM will have done little to dispel. This raises the possibility of the US response to EMU following a similar path to its response to the SEM programme. The US neglected both the original

Cockfield White Paper of 1985 and the SEA when it was agreed in 1986. It sat up and took notice only in 1988, when the implementation of the SEM programme began to impinge upon its interests directly. The spectre of 'fortress Europe' then emerged and was not put to rest until after much work had been done clarifying the real impact of the SEM programme. There was also a more or less accurate perception that the EC had given no thought to the implications of the 1992 programme for the rest of the world, and that the SEM programme reflected an introverted view on the part of the EC.

A similar response to EMU is quite possible. As with the SEA in 1987, the changes launched by the Maastricht Treaty, and the critical agreement on EMU, had virtually no coverage in the American press and made little impact on the US political scene.[20] But American scepticism underestimates the political commitment to European integration and EMU on the part of most member states. There is still a possibility that the 1999 target for a single currency will generate the momentum for change that the 1992 programme did. The convergence criteria required are being used by governments to bring about structural changes, such as the Italian privatization programme, which have not been possible in the past without the added incentive of wishing to be inside EMU. This may well enable member states that currently do not seem likely to be able to meet the convergence criteria to take the steps needed at least to be moving in the right direction.

At the time of writing (August 1992) many member states are striving to stick with the tight discipline implied by their membership of the EMS and the convergence criteria, despite high costs in terms of high interest rates and stagnant economies. These pressures are especially intense in Britain because it joined the ERM just as the Bundesbank was putting on the brakes in an attempt to contain inflation created by the transfers from west to east Germany. The period 1992–3 will be crucial for the future of EMU. If the EC withstands the pressures created by the recession, and preserves the commitment of the majority of member states to continue to follow policies aimed at convergence, then the likelihood of a majority of member states entering into a single currency by the turn of the century will have increased; if not, US sceptics, as well as the many doubters elsewhere, would have been proved correct.

Whatever happens on EMU, the question of coordination of policies within the EC will become more rather than less important as time goes on. If there have been difficulties developing coherent trade policies, how will the EC deal with the coordination of trade, monetary, exchange-rate and fiscal policies that would be required if the EC were to become an active player in the international economy in the conventional sense? The problems will increase because competence for these policy areas will not be brought under one roof except that of the European Council. The Commission will negotiate on trade (including such issues as environmental and competition policies) on the basis of the Council's mandate as at present. The European Central Bank will determine monetary policy. ECOFIN, the European Council of Economic and Finance Ministers, will decide on 'formal' exchange-rate regimes, with the ECB dealing with 'informal' arrangements. There is a question here as to whether 'Plaza Accord'-type of arrangements are formal or not. Fiscal policy will still be in the hands of the national finance ministers. As if this were not complex enough, any use of the economic instruments in the pursuit of foreign policy objectives will be in the hands of the foreign ministers, unless there is agreement that the area of activity concerned should be one of joint action within the meaning of the CFSP provisions of Maastricht.

Policy coordination in the US

Although there is a single powerful executive branch in the USA, it has not been without its difficulties in terms of policy coordination.[21] There are also inter-agency coordination issues. In the 1940s and 1950s the State Department fulfilled an overall coordinating role for US international economic policy. As, however, the impact of the international economy on the US grew, more and more departments of government began to assume an active interest in such policies. By the 1970s the State Department's role had been significantly reduced. There has been a progressive fragmentation of decisionmaking among Commerce, Agriculture, Treasury and other departments. In the field of trade policy the Special Trade Representative's Office, later the US Trade Representative's Office (USTR), was established to coordinate trade negotiations. In addition, there has been a progressive shift in power away from the executive to Congress, especially on trade policy measures. Congress has always had constitutional powers to determine the commercial policy of the Union, but it had delegated many of these to the executive branch. With successive pieces of trade legislation in 1973, 1979 and 1988, Congress has narrowed the discretionary powers of the administration by codifying more and more aspects of international trade and investment policy and limiting the administration's discretion when implementing the legislation. Since Congress must endorse the results of trade negotiations, such as the Uruguay Round or the NAFTA, the administration's ability to deliver on multilateral agreements is controlled by Congress:

US negotiators are effectively negotiating with the USA's trade partners and Congress at the same time.

The difficulties of delivering are, as noted above, further complicated by the fact that the individual states play increasingly important roles in international commerce. This is again especially the case in trade and investment issues. The administration retains more autonomy when it comes to foreign and security policy. The new problem that the end of the cold war brings for the US is that of the increasing linkage between security and economic issues. This increases the importance of economic instruments and thus the leverage Congress has over policy. Broadly speaking, however, the US retains an ability to initiate policies and to act that cannot be matched by the Community at present and is unlikely to be matched for some time to come, even if member states overcome their antipathy towards the centralization of policy formulation and implementation that would be needed for a coherent EC foreign economic policy. Chapter 2 has discussed the gap between the evolution of policy concepts and the ability of the US to follow through. In trade policy there has been an equivalent gap, in that throughout the 1980s it was the USA which launched most initiatives in multilateral trade negotiations, but, as the negotiations advanced, doubts about its ability to follow through – in the sense of Congress passing implementing legislation – have grown.

Bilateral coordination: towards the Transatlantic Declaration
There have been bilateral contacts between the EC and the US for many years. These existed almost from the outset between the Commission and the US administration, between the US and European Political Cooperation (EPC) since the early 1970s, and between the European Parliament and the US House of Representatives since the EP was directly elected.

Developments within Europe during 1988 and 1989 led to efforts on the part of both the United States and the EC (member states, Commission and European Parliament) to strengthen the links between the Community and the US. In early 1989 the President of the Commission, Jacques Delors, called for a more structured relationship between the Community and the US. The initial response to this from Washington was 'very sympathetic', but there was no formal response until the Bush administration had completed its review of US foreign policy. In a speech at Boston University in May 1989, just before leaving for his first trip to Europe as President, Mr Bush spoke of the US being 'ready to develop new mechanisms with the European Community and member states on political and global issues, from strengthening the forces of democracy in the third world, to managing regional tensions, to putting an end to the divisions of Europe.'[22]

The motivation behind this US initiative seems to have been threefold: first, there was a desire to articulate the support for greater European integration; second, if the EC was going to play a more important political role, the US wished to ensure it could influence EC decisions; and, third, there existed a desire to counteract the negative impact of the heated exchanges over fortress Europe and somewhat petty trade issues such as the beef hormones dispute. In meetings during 1989, Bush and Delors agreed that efforts should be made to ensure regular meetings between the two in Brussels and Washington. Work also began on what would ultimately become the Transatlantic Declaration.

In December 1989 Secretary Baker, in his Berlin speech, proposed 'that the United States and the European Community work together to achieve, whether in treaty or some other form, a significantly strengthened set of institutional and consultational links'.[23] In a subsequent 'ministerial meeting' with the Commission it was decided to hold such ministerial meetings in their own right rather than when the US Secretary of State happened to be in Brussels following a NATO meeting. It was also decided to return to holding meetings every six months during 1990, and to alternate between Washington and Brussels. The Commission stressed that there would be more visits by Commissioners to deal with specific issues, and a string of Commissioners visited Washington during 1990 to discuss competition, R&D and economic policy. These meetings were in addition to regular meetings of trade officials.

The Council was working on parallel measures to strengthen links on political issues. In February 1990 the President of the Council, Charles Haughey, proposed more formal arrangements for regular meetings between the Council President and the US President to provide 'overall guidance for the relationship', and an institutionalization of biannual meetings between EC foreign ministers and the US Secretary of State to give 'a better overall structure and direction to the wide variety of existing contacts and discussions' and 'a new framework for enhanced political and economic ties between the Community and the US'.[24]

During the summer of 1990 negotiations began in earnest on whether there should be a formal agreement between the EC and the US, and if so what it would look like. The German foreign minister, Hans-Dietrich Genscher, favoured some form of treaty or declaration. The Commission was not enthusiastic about the idea of a treaty, because the Community had just begun the intergovernmental negotiations on political and eco-

60

nomic union, and it was felt that it would be best to wait and see what emerged from these before concluding a treaty with the US. It was, in particular, not clear what role, if any, the EC would have in foreign and security policy. This view prevailed, and negotiations began on the wording of a declaration, with the option of a treaty left open. The negotiations soon ran into difficulties over the efforts of parts of the US administration to include a commitment on the Uruguay Round. The State Department was coordinating but not dictating the negotiations. For its part, the EC wanted to include reference to the need for freer trade at both national and state levels, something neither the State Department nor the administration could deliver. The EC also wished to include reference for the need for financial stability, by which it meant the need for the US to exercise greater budgetary discipline. The US administration opposed this because the Treasury wanted no commitment to discuss US fiscal or monetary policies with the Community. In a variation of the 'seat at the table' debate initiated in the context of the 1992 programme, the US sought the means of influencing EC policies by proposing meetings of 'the Thirteen'. This was seen by the EC, and especially the French, as wholly unacceptable.

To reach agreement it was necessary to drop the contentious issues, with the result that the final text contained little in the way of commitments. It set out the common goals of support for 'democracy, safeguarding peace and the pursuit of policies aimed at achieving a sound world economy marked by sustained economic growth with low inflation, a high level of unemployment, equitable social conditions, in a framework of international stability'. Economic cooperation stopped well short of any new commitments on macro policy and focused on 'support for further steps towards liberalization, transparency, and the implementation of GATT and OECD principles concerning both trade in goods and services and investment' and 'further development of the dialogue on non-tariff barriers, competition policy, transport, standards, telecoms and high technology'. Among other objectives was the promotion of 'market principles', to help developing countries and to provide adequate support, with others, for central and Eastern Europe. The political goals included efforts to address the transnational challenges of tackling terrorism, narcotics and international crime. There was reference to the need to protect the environment, both internationally and domestically, by integrating environmental and economic goals and, in the field of (soft) security, preventing the proliferation of nuclear arms, chemical and biological weapons and missile technology.

The differences over the drafting resulted in much of the political impact of the Declaration being lost, since it could not be signed, as envisaged, at the time of the Conference on Security and Cooperation in Europe (CSCE) in Paris in November 1990. One thing the Declaration did do, however, was to confirm and formalize the institutional links between the EC and the US that had been worked out during the previous year between the Commission and Council, on the one hand, and the US administration on the other. These were as follows:

- *Presidential level*   Biannual consultations between the Presidents of the Council and Commission and the US President;
- *Ministerial level*   Biannual consultations between the EC foreign ministers, Commissioners, and the US Secretary of State;
- *Troika foreign ministers*   Consultation between the Presidency Foreign Minister or the Troika (the current presidency of the Council and the preceding and following ones) and the US Secretary of State, to take place on an ad-hoc basis generally at the beginning of each new EC presidency;
- *Commission*   Biannual consultation between the Commission and the US government at Cabinet level;
- *Political Directors*   Briefings, as already existed, by the Presidency to US Representatives on EPC meetings at the ministerial level (biannual briefings for Political Directors plus more frequent ad-hoc expert meetings); and
- *Congress and European Parliament*   A welcome for the joint meetings decided upon by Congress and the European Parliament.[25]

Despite the sentiments in the Declaration, on most political issues contacts have been between the US administration and the individual member states. Washington's attitude has been that when in doubt talk to the member states. As the US Ambassador to the European Communities, Mr Alfred Kingon, put it in 1989, 'Washington takes the lead from the member states, if they say foreign policy or monetary policy will in future be a Community issue the US will talk to Brussels'.[26] Even on issues covered by Community competence, the US has not held back from lobbying individual countries, especially when there were clear   differences of interest between the member states. In areas in which Community competence is not clear-cut, or when the Commission is seeking a greater role, US lobbying of member states has created controversy within the EC. For example, US lobbying in telecommunications initially targeted the national governments and regulatory bodies, a move which upset the Commission because it was in the process of formulating Community policy in the sector.

In addition to official channels of communication, there is a whole network of unofficial channels between the US and the various European countries. The private sector is particularly important in the trade and economic field, the main channel being multinational companies which operate on both sides of the Atlantic. Formal links between private sector interest groups have tended to be less effective, although they do take place through such bodies as the US Business Round Table or the Council for International Business, in the US, and through UNICE and the European Roundtable of Industrialists in the EC. One of the problems with private sector links is that here also there are systemic differences. The US tends to rely on ad-hoc coalitions of companies, while the Europeans have a more structured system based on sectoral trade associations and national or EC confederations of industry.

Multilateral coordination

There are two possible views about the strength of the Community in international policy coordination. On the one hand, it could be argued that the numerical superiority of 'the Europeans' in international organizations gives them a disproportionate influence when they coordinate their inputs. For example, there are four EC members in the G7. This means that when they coordinate their positions they can shape the outcome, and can certainly frustrate any US attempts to form coalitions with only those of the four that share their view. The Americans tend to refer to this as 'caucusing' and see it as having a detrimental effect on the G7 process (as well as US interests). In Houston in June 1990 the US administration was unhappy about such caucusing, which prevented France being isolated on the agricultural issue in the declaration covering the Uruguay Round. On the other hand, the absence of a single EC voice is seen by some as weakening the role of the Community in international fora. Of these – the GATT, OECD, G7, IMF, IBRD, not to mention the security-related bodies, the US Security Council, NATO, CSCE – the EC is a signatory only of the GATT. The member states negotiate in all the other bodies.

Clearly one must be careful to differentiate between the influence of the Community and the 'European' countries participating; but, as the EC assumes more competencies, the kind of issues that have arisen in the consideration of the Uruguay Round in the G7 summits will occur in other fora. In other words, there will be more areas in which the EC holds a common position but has a multiple voice in international fora. This will be particularly important in fora such as the OECD. After enlargement of the EC, Community member states will form the overwhelming majority of this organization, unless, as is contemplated, membership is extended to countries such as Korea. In the IMF, a single voice for the EC would mean less voting power, since the combined EC quota, and thus the EC vote, would be based on extra-EC trade and not on the trade of each individual member state, which includes intra-EC trade. On the other hand, the absence of a single EC voice means that there will be opportunities for the US to build coalitions with those member states which share its view.[27]

A central question is whether a single EC voice is going to enhance international coordination. In trade policy, as noted, a single EC voice has meant that the Community has tended to internalize part of the multilateral process. The need for a consensus among the Twelve has also arguably made it less flexible. In the field of monetary policy, it is possible that a common voice will make coordination less easy for similar reasons. Once the European Central Bank has agreed on a monetary policy appropriate for the EC, it will be harder to make changes in order to accommodate the interests of others. The ECB is, after all, supposed to be independent, and thus not subject to pressure even from the national governments of the member states, let alone third countries. Equally, once the Council or the ECB has agreed a common position on exchange rates, it will be difficult to adjust this in order to reflect the concerns of others. Thus a single EC voice could reduce the degree of flexibility in international economic policy coordination and with it the ability of the US to form coalitions with different European countries.

Conclusions

In discussing the respective roles of the EC and the US in the international economy, we have attempted to consider both current conditions and the implications of possible future developments, such as the realization of EMU. This is necessary because, even if it remains less than certain that EMU will succeed, the potential implications for the role of the EC in the world economy and its implications for the USA are significant. When compared with the events and trends in approaches to political order (see Chapter 4), many of the processes discussed here are long-term and structural in nature, rather than leading to short-term upheavals or crises; none the less, the linkages between the two areas are often intense, and awareness of their policy implications has grown markedly during the past decade. The issues explored lead to the following conclusions:

- First, the broad conclusion is that the EC has increased its economic muscle relative to the USA. The US remains a considerable force and one that is more than able to do considerable damage to the international economy if domestic pressures get the upper hand. But its ability to shape the multilateral and international economic order has been declining for some time. The revival of the EC has helped to bring about a cognitive shift in the minds of many Americans to a greater recognition of this fact. None the less, the USA can be expected to exercise its considerable economic weight in a potentially volatile manner as it responds to domestic frustrations or pressures.
- Second, the Community remains more effective as a process than as an actor. Its strengths lie in the area of international economic interdependence, where the 'Community' approach, based on a willingness to accommodate systemic differences, offers better prospects for the international system than the US approach, which still follows traditional harmonization-based lines. But the Community is weaker than the US when it comes to articulating and launching policy initiatives. This combination of factors has tended – and seems likely to continue – to result in frustration on the part of the US. On the one hand, the Americans often feel that they cannot break into the EC policymaking process. This frustration has led to requests for a 'seat at the table' and an interest in bilateral consultation procedures as a means of trying to influence the internal EC decisionmaking process. On the other hand, many American observers miss a more active EC and there is a general expectation that as the EC builds economic muscle it should also assume a more active role on the international stage. But this is a role that the EC is unlikely to fill and quite possibly should not attempt to. If the EC approach is more effective as a process of dealing with integration it may be better for this process to be allowed to work, rather than expect the EC to assume the role of a conventional economic superpower.
- Third, neither the Community nor the United States conforms to the model of a monolithic regional bloc, but both contain tendencies which are a challenge to the multilateral order. Although both are rhetorically committed to the preservation or the enhancement of multilateralism, it may be that the tension between the search for

multilateralism and the temptations of introversion or aggressive unilateralism will produce further conflicts and misunderstandings, which will be exacerbated by the growth of market and policy interdependence.

– Finally, there are distinct differences and potential problems between the Community and the USA in the area of policy coordination. Both face the issue of reconciling economic interpenetration with the need for internal policy coherence. In the case of the Community, the limitations on its ability to produce a coordinated foreign economic policy will become more apparent as the scope of Community competence increases. In the case of the USA, problems arising from the separation of powers at federal level are compounded by the intervention of state-level and other forces, which are given added impact by the intensification of interdependence and interpenetration. A number of these influences make themselves felt in the attempt to further international coordination, whether multilateral or bilateral. As a result, there is intense and growing contact, but it is not always clear in which direction or with what purpose such contacts are moving.

One of the more general conclusions of this chapter is that the mutual involvement of the EC and the United States in the world economic order must also be seen in the context of their increasing entanglement with the problem of political order in Europe and beyond. This is the subject of Chapter 4.

4

THE CHANGING POLITICAL ORDER

The United States and the European Community are confronted by a number of major challenges centring upon the impact of political change and the search for political order. On the one hand, these challenges are focused by developments in a number of sensitive arenas: the former Soviet Union, the 'new Germany', the new states system in central and eastern Europe, and the new 'arc of crisis', extending from the eastern Mediterranean to central Asia. At the same time, these and other changes intersect with a number of uncertainties about the changing international agenda, the instruments of influence and the institutional context of transatlantic dealings. In this chapter, we are concerned both with the changing landscape and structure of international order and with the policy responses of the USA and the EC. The aim is to provide an account of issues and events as they have emerged during the early 1990s, and to pull out from this account important pointers to the components of, and the necessary conditions for, a new Euro-Atlantic partnership.[1]

The chapter is structured around three key areas:

(1) The ways in which the USA and the EC have responded to the collapse of the Soviet Union, the emergence of the new Germany and the politics of the new European states system, particularly the crisis in Yugoslavia.
(2) American and European responses to the Gulf war and the emergence of a new 'arc of crisis', extending from the eastern Mediterranean through the Gulf to central Asia and constituting a major test of the notion of a New World Order.
(3) The ways in which the USA and the Community have handled the

new political challenges in such domains as immigration, weapons proliferation and the human environment, and the ways in which they have approached the need for a new institutional framework in the politics of Atlantic relations.

The argument in general can be simply stated: the response of both the USA and the Community to the challenges of a changing international political order has been patchy and uncertain, with the danger of being overwhelmed by events, and with the additional possibility of major misunderstandings between the two Euro-Atlantic 'partners'. But this does not mean that US/EC relations have broken down or been submerged by the forces of change: one of the key features of the new era in US/European security relations has been the capacity of leaderships and institutions to respond incrementally to cover the potential gaps in understanding and policy. Whether this kind of response is likely to be effective or appropriate in the longer term is a question to which we shall return explicitly in Chapter 5.

Coping with the collapse of the Soviet Union

The overturning of one of the major 'givens' in Atlantic relations, the presence and threatening posture of the USSR, has raised a series of taxing dilemmas for both the United States and the European Community. One issue has been that of recognition: just who should western policies be aimed at, who should be accorded legitimacy and who should be granted the attention of western diplomacy? A connected issue is that of aid and assistance: assuming that appropriate targets can be identified, what are the responsibilities of the western allies for the provision of aid, and how should such aid be processed? The question of aid merges into another, that of leverage: how, in the near-chaos of the ex-Soviet Union, is effective political influence to be exerted, and who has the better chance of achieving such influence? For the Euro-Atlantic partners, these issues are not merely those of pragmatic policymaking and implementation: they also raise questions about the terms on which future transatlantic relations are to be conducted.

The fall of the Berlin Wall and its aftermath during 1990 added new dimensions to a set of East/West relations that had been inching towards some form of normality during the 1980s, but had nevertheless been uneven and often halting. Prior to the revolutions of 1989 and 1990, relations between the United States and the east European countries that were members of the Council for Mutual Economic Assistance (CMEA) had been strictly governed by the larger context of US/Soviet relations. The echoes of the early 1980s, with sanctions against both the USSR and its client regimes, meant that the disentangling of new realities from long-standing perceptions was a difficult task. For the Community and its members, the task was even more complex: the spectrum of interests and existing connections ranged from the close involvement of the west Germans to the relative distance of the British and others. But the Community had the foundations for a rapid development of economic linkages, both at the national and at the Community level; negotiations may have been slow during the 1980s, and the growth of trade distinctly patchy, but the links had been made. The unlocking of new forces and new opportunities during 1989 and 1990 thus found the EC ready not only to respond but also to present itself as a model for the growth of pluralist capitalism in the East.[2]

It was apparent at an early stage not only that the Community could and would act to support the east Europeans, but also that the USA faced problems in responding rapidly to the transformation. Whereas the EC had existing agreements with CMEA countries, and had the impetus both from Brussels and from national capitals to become involved, the Americans confronted a series of domestic and financial constraints on a rapid increase in their engagement. As a result, during 1990 the Community was able to establish new aid programmes such as PHARE, and to intensify contacts between national bureaucracies and experts in an effort to support the transition to democracy. At the same time, Washington explicitly acknowledged the leading responsibility of the EC in coordinating aid to the former CMEA countries through the G24. When the European Bank for Reconstruction and Development was set up, it was the EC that took a major role in its constitution and funding, although the USA was the largest single-country contributor to the Bank's funding. It was not clear, though, how far the leading role of the Community could be extended beyond the economic and administrative into the political domain, or how far the interests of individual EC members such as Germany would come to dominate against the collective interests of the Community as a whole.[3]

Once the initial euphoria occasioned by the 'liberation' of eastern Europe had passed in early 1990, it became apparent that the new nationalisms of the Warsaw Pact countries were not the only yearnings for freedom in the Soviet bloc. Rapidly, it transpired that both the 'captive nations' of the Baltic region and a number of long-suppressed separatist movements in the Soviet Union itself were at issue. Such pressures came up against the feeling both in the United States and in western Europe that Mikhail Gorbachev and the process of perestroika should be preserved; and one of the central themes in European/American relations for the next eighteen months was to be the interplay between the desire for stability in the USSR and the handling of ultimately irrepressible demands for change. During 1990, the tendency to caution was buttressed by the need to rely upon the Soviet Union for essential intergovernmental agreements, particularly those in respect of German unification and further arms reductions. Although there were decided variations between the postures adopted by different European leaderships, the general tendency was clear. Baltic independence was to be placed firmly within the context of the need to deal with Moscow, while unrest in the Soviet Union itself was viewed through the prism of the need for order and the preservation of responsible government. The pay-off was tangible and certainly not negligible: the unification of Germany within NATO, the bolstering of the CSCE process and the conclusion of the Conventional Forces in Europe (CFE) accords at the end of 1990.

By the end of 1990 also, the question of Soviet stability was placed firmly into the context of the New World Order as expressed in responses to the Gulf crisis. This had two major effects on US policy in particular. On the one hand, the support, or at least the acquiescence, of Moscow was essential for effective action by the coalition against Iraq. At the same time, the demands of coalition management and military deployment in the Gulf were a severe distraction both for the Americans and for the Europeans.[4] We shall deal later with the implications of these events for Euro-Atlantic relations, but it is important here to note the ways in which political change in the Soviet Union became hostage to broader forces of international and Atlantic relations. Although the momentum of arms reduction proposals was maintained through measures announced by President Bush and then taken up by Moscow, there was an indefinable feeling that the European order had taken a back seat in Washington. This was not shared, for example, by Germany or France, which continued to press for increases in aid to the Soviet Union both bilaterally and through the EC; on the other hand, the Thatcher government in Britain maintained a resolute adherence to the American position that Gorbachev should be supported firmly but conditionally.

During early 1991, though, it became apparent that the western commitment to maintenance of the Soviet regime was under severe strain. The hardening of the Soviet line towards the Baltic states, leading eventually to the use of force as well as economic blockades, was symptomatic both of the pressures for the break-up of the Union and of the beleaguered status of the Moscow regime. Differences of view within the EC about the desirability of sending more than essential humanitarian assistance to Moscow were sharpened, while in the USA there appeared to be major obstacles to any increase in the level of assistance. The problem for Washington seemed to have two central components: on the one hand, the Bush administration was acutely conscious of its limited ability to influence events in the Soviet Union, particularly in the context of the war in the Gulf; on the other, it was equally aware of its inability to influence Congress and to 'sell' aid to the East at a time of domestic recession.[5]

In this context, the use of force against the Baltic states in early 1991 served as a catalyst for tensions both within the EC and between the Community and Washington. Although trade negotiations were suspended by the Community, and there were threats of a freeze to aid, the prevailing line was cautious. At the same time, the Americans were impaled on the dilemma of support for Gorbachev and increasing domestic demands for strong measures in support of the Baltics. Those who implied that German policies were a form of appeasement directed towards Moscow failed to recognize both the continuing imperatives of the post-unification period for the Bonn government and their own reluctance to force a rupture with the Soviet regime. By the middle of 1991, Mr Gorbachev was being offered the incentive of attending the London summit, but in some ways this appears to have been a poisoned chalice. Within a month of his appearance in London, and only three weeks after the Moscow summit with President Bush, the Soviet leader was successively imprisoned, restored and humiliated by a combination of the old and the new forces for change in the USSR.

The abortive coup of August 1991 was a watershed not only for the process of change in the Soviet Union but also for the perceptions and responses of the western allies. President Bush's conception of a New World Order rested heavily on the assumption that responsible and legitimate governments could come to accommodations about the forces of change and disruption, and this was certainly a central element of American support for the Gorbachev government. The oscillations of 1990 in Moscow, between liberation and repression, and the increasing evidence of instability at the core of the Soviet system, had caused misgivings in Washington but no large-scale reassessment of policy. Indeed, the need to pin the USSR down to desirable agreements in arms

71

control and other areas had given the Americans considerable incentives to stick with the established order. At a stroke, in August, the Soviet Union was transformed from a legitimate partner in the New World Order to an unknown quantity. The effects were felt not only in Washington but also in the EC and in Euro-Atlantic relations.[6]

Immediate responses to the coup on both sides of the Atlantic were both cautious and ambivalent, reflecting the widespread reluctance to admit that Gorbachev was doomed, while at the same time attempting to take stock of the putative successor regime. From the American point of view, the priority seemed to be the preservation of gains in the arms reduction context; although there was a feeling that the failure to provide more aid to the Soviet regime might have contributed to its downfall, there was also a search for a possible accommodation with the new forces. A similar tension was apparent in the EC, with the French particularly willing to contemplate relations with the new regime and the Germans anxious to preserve the gains of the last two years. One positive result was the speeding up of EC negotiations on association with the east European countries, the so-called 'Europe Agreements', and a greater willingness to make economic concessions in the cause of political order. There was less certainty in west European responses to east European demands for security collaboration, which raised important questions of institutional competence and interests (see below).

The defeat of the coup and the emergence of Boris Yeltsin as the central political force in a disintegrating Soviet Union forced both the Europeans and the United States to take stock of their positions, and laid bare some of the contradictions to which they had led. A cascade of new demands now followed: for the recognition of the Baltics (led by the Community, with the United States at a small but significant distance), for massive increases in aid (led by the Germans, with all others in the rear and with the Americans still unable to unlock the purse-strings), for urgent measures to handle the military and especially the nuclear consequences of the break-up (led by the United States, with new calls for massive arms reductions and the elimination of tactical nuclear weapons in Europe).

From the end of August 1991, the central trends in EC and US responses to the Soviet break-up diverged quite markedly. On the side of the Europeans – and the Community in particular – the emphasis was on aid and assistance, with the Germans in the lead. A major conditioning factor in this concern was the heavy exposure of many European countries to debts incurred by the former Soviet authorities, but for some a more immediate fear was of mass movement of Soviet population to the

West. Although the Americans subscribed to such efforts in general terms, it was apparent that they could not or would not muster massive resources in support of the European initiative. This could be rationalized as a prudent emphasis on the technical aspects of Soviet (or post-Soviet) economic reform, but it increasingly came to appear a threadbare excuse. When in December 1991 Secretary of State James Baker took the initiative in calling a multilateral conference on aid to the former Soviet Union, it was taken in bad part by many European leaders, who interpreted it as an attempt to invoke an outdated hegemonic role for the United States. The conference itself, in January 1992, managed to patch up some of the emerging conflicts between the two sides of the Atlantic, but it was significant that the follow-up meeting was to be held in Europe, with the Europeans playing a more prominent part. As it transpired, the significant development of spring 1992 was the growing role of the G7 and the IMF as channels for agreements and their implementation; but the $24 billion aid package of April still could not conceal the tensions in the American position.[7]

In fact, on the American side, the main concern continued to be the control of the massive Soviet nuclear arsenal. The prospect of anything up to 30,000 footloose nuclear warheads spread across potentially warring successor republics was enough to concentrate the mind of Washington wonderfully, and immense efforts were bent to ensure not only that existing agreements should be observed but that new and more ambitious reductions should be achieved. As with the case of economic and humanitarian aid, however, the problem was finding authoritative partners and concluding binding arrangements with them. We shall deal below with the proliferation issues arising from this context; here it should merely be stressed that the central priority of American policy towards the former Soviet Union remained the control and containment of the military fall-out from the break-up. Although it would be too crude to draw a definite line between the European concern with aid and the American concern with containment, the difference in emphasis is certainly identifiable at many points.[8]

Flowing from these central differences in emphasis were important tensions between European and American diplomatic activities. For the Europeans, it was logical at an early stage to consider the opening of relations with the successor republics, and in this the lead was taken again by the Germans. By the end of 1991, it was only a short step for many European leaderships to establish formal relations, and for the Community under German leadership to explore the possibility of joint representation in such republics as Ukraine. Although the Americans had recognized Ukraine and other republics, their focus on the need for central control of the ex-Soviet nuclear forces produced an ambivalence which was bound to condition their actions. It remained the case, however, that only the United States had the technical capacity and the military standing to negotiate authoritatively in this area.

It would be too neat to assert that the differing priorities and capacities of the Europeans and the Americans had led by mid-1992 to an effective division of labour in dealing with the former Soviet Union. On the other hand, it is clear that the predominant emphasis of the Europeans on issues of recognition, of aid and of economic stabilization acted as a counterpoint to the American focus on order, on control of nuclear and other weapons, and on the preservation of the gains from a decade of arms reduction efforts. By early 1992, the concerns had broadened to encompass the potential for conflict and even open warfare between successor republics in the Caucasus and central Asia, most clearly in the escalating conflict between Armenia and Azerbaijan. Here, the Europeans and the Americans shared a concern which led them to emphasize the role of the CSCE and the emerging North Atlantic Cooperation Council (NACC). The first of these bodies could apply tests of acceptability and confer at least some legitimacy; the second, implicitly under American leadership, could tackle the process of demilitarization and civilianization which was increasingly central to the prospects for order in the ruins of the Soviet empire.

Adapting to the 'New Germany'
The position and status of Germany has always been central to relations between the United States and Europe. For the Atlantic Alliance, the extent to which Germany has been westward- or eastward-looking has been a constant if often muted concern. For the European Community, the connected tension between 'European Germany' and 'German Europe' has emerged with greater insistence as first the Federal Republic, and then a united Germany, has made its presence felt. In both the Atlantic and the European context, the issue of German passivity or assertiveness, and the direction of German policies, have come to mean more and have acquired more insistence as the economic and political weight of the Federal Republic has been augmented. The process through which a united Germany emerged during 1990, and the ways in which German influence has been used since unification, are thus central to the

development of Euro-Atlantic relations during the 1990s. Not least do they raise questions about the institutional framework for European/ American relations, given the central place occupied by Germany in any 'Euro-Atlantic architecture'.[9]

The process of German unification engaged the concentrated attention of both the European Community and American policymakers during 1990. For the Community, in a sense, the issue was one of long historical standing: from its earliest stages, European integration has been a mechanism for containing not only a resurgent Germany but also moderating the fears and apprehensions of the French in particular. Not just the French, but the British as well, had an entirely understandable concern that the 'new Germany' should be tied into the network of institutional arrangements centring upon but not confined to the European Community. This concern was to a degree shared by the USA and the Bush administration, but there was in Washington a more explicit tendency to view the German issue within the context of US/Soviet relations. In this context, the salient institutional arrangements were not only those of the Community, but also those of the CSCE and NATO: the former provided a set of general constraints and normative principles for constraining the move to unification; the latter, an indispensable means of leverage and positional influence for the USA in its relations with Bonn. Substance was added to these American concerns by the intimate relationship between the unification process and the political and security position in eastern Europe and the Soviet Union. Mishandling of the German problem could lead to setbacks in the opening up of the Warsaw Pact and the reform of the Soviet superpower.

As it transpired, in many ways the role of the western allies was that of accommodation rather than shaping or constraint. The pressure for unification, and the momentum it generated during 1990, were so intense that the main concern of the allies was to find ways of adjusting to the unfolding reality. This is not to argue that the Community or NATO played no role, or that the concerns of the British and the French were of no account: rather, it is to point out that the initiative lay with the Germans, and also that the key negotiating concessions were made by the Soviet regime during the summer of 1990, when they agreed to the prospect of a united Germany within the Western alliance. Not for the first or the last time under George Bush, Washington played an important role by accommodating and providing the diplomatic context for important agreements. The decisions that led to the 'two plus four' talks in February 1990, the forging of a common position on German membership in NATO, and the provision of guarantees essential to Soviet acceptance of that membership in May and June, can all be seen as the reflection of American initiatives.[10]

The British, on the other hand, were the most reluctant to adjust, with Prime Minister Margaret Thatcher maintaining her caution about the united Germany until the last. Although Mrs Thatcher's stance could not be taken to represent that of the British government as a whole, she represented a strong strand within a general line of policy emphasizing the NATO connection above all others. Indeed, it was clear in the summer of 1990 that there were tensions not only between London and other Community capitals but also between London and Washington, where the desire to accommodate without making undue concessions was central. The French, as in earlier times, placed a strong emphasis on the use of European integration in the cause of containing Germany, and this was pregnant with implications for the later debates on political union leading up to the Maastricht Treaty. During 1990 and 1991, beginning with the Mitterrand/Kohl initiative of March 1990, the French and the Germans produced a series of initiatives aimed at shaping the agenda for debate on common foreign and security policies in the Community, often in distinct tension with the British position, but it is open to argument how much the Franco-German line shaped the eventual outcome at Maastricht, let alone how much the French line actively shaped German policies.[11]

The unification process made one thing quite clear: that the 'new Germany' would maintain a strong concern with the affairs of the Soviet Union and eastern Europe, while balancing this with its commitment to the EC and to NATO. Given that in the post-unification phase a major feature of the political and security context was the fracturing of the Soviet bloc, the problem for German diplomacy and for the Western alliance was clear. We have already noted the ways in which German priorities shaped evolving attitudes towards the Soviet Union and the Baltic states during 1990 and 1991; importantly, in many instances it was the Germans who could supply the economic and diplomatic muscle to sustain or to modify the status quo. Their position as the major donors of aid to eastern Europe and the Soviet Union (and then to its successor republics), and their historical links to many of the areas striving for liberation, gave them a special position of leverage. This leverage in itself was a matter of concern to other states in western Europe, including fellow members of the Community that had less firmly settled convictions and less purchase on the problems of the East. The German concern to lead in establishing a new order in the East, or to contain damaging changes, was not at all abstract: the destabilization of the ex-Warsaw Pact countries, or the emergence of civil strife in economically weakened new states, raised the spectre of mass involuntary movements of population which would only add to the already large influx of migrants into the Federal Republic. From the American point of view, the possibility of establishing a new partnership with a united Germany was given some emphasis during 1990 and 1991, but the growing domestic preoccupations of both the Kohl and the Bush administrations, as well as the frictions over eastern policy, saw no real consolidation of the position during 1992.[12]

Germany has thus emerged as a prime mover in the establishment of new mechanisms for handling conflict in the new Europe of the 1990s. What is notable about this emergence, though, is that it makes the maximum possible use of multilateral frameworks. At one level, this is a self-serving device: the Germans either wish to escape the odium of taking unilateral restrictive measures (for example, on immigration) or want to avoid being identified as overly assertive or expansionist. But at another level, there is clear evidence that the Kohl government and many ordinary Germans have a substantial loyalty to the existing multilateral framework, and to the legitimacy afforded by its institutions. We shall deal later with the institutional framework itself, but the key point to be emphasized here is that the Germans have chosen to operate well within the established institutional structures.[13]

This does not mean that the Germans have not influenced the shape and the functioning of the institutions in which they are entangled. In the case of the EC, the effects of the 'new Germany' have been profound: the move to economic and to political union is in many respects a direct expression of the need to accommodate a new and potent force, and the German insistence on the interdependence of the two strands has been central to their development. Not only this, but the German position – whether assertive or ambiguous – has shaped EC policies on the Soviet Union and its collapse, on the Gulf war, and on the conflict in what was Yugoslavia. Some would no doubt argue that the new diplomacy of the Community, including its criteria for the recognition of new states and its readiness to use economic coercive measures, are a direct result of German assertiveness. In many ways this is correct, although often the effect has been felt through the anticipatory or defensive moves of Britain and France rather than through open German domination. Certainly, the desire to act collectively in the presence of an implied German threat to act unilaterally has become a leitmotif of some recent Community actions, but this has also been conditioned by the often intense debates in Germany itself about the constitutional implications of the use of sanctions or force. In this respect, it is still open to question whether EC policies in the 1990s will be characterized by the effective exertion of German dominance or the paradox of 'power without purpose' which could be seen as resulting from German domestic uncertainty.[14]

No less profound have been the effects of German policies for the broader Euro-Atlantic framework, in particular the CSCE and NATO. One clear priority of American policy in the unification process was to contain the united Germany within NATO. This was indeed achieved, but it is open to question whether it was as a result of American efforts or of a more complex mix of western and Soviet actions. The rapid development of a new military balance in central Europe since the unification of Germany has given the Bonn government not only a central stake in the continued life of NATO but also a more prominent place in the military structure, given the projected denuclearization of central Europe and the draw-down of allied forces, most notably those of the USA itself. Alongside the classical NATO framework, the Germans have attempted to play a complex balancing game between the existing NATO structure, the new mechanisms of European Union and the broader CSCE framework, and this is not by any means an easy balance to preserve. On the one hand, the French have made every effort to recruit the Germans to an ambitious version of EC security collaboration, with the implied effect of separation from the North Atlantic focus at some indefinite future date. At the same time, the British and the Americans have stressed the continued need for NATO and for the German commitment to it. Alongside both of these influences, the importance of the CSCE as a structure for civilized behaviour between new states in a new Europe has been constantly underlined, as has its lack of real muscle. Given the uncertainties already noted about the German position in relation to sanctions or force, the relevance of these structures and their limitations has become even more central.[15]

The events of 1990-92 have clearly reflected not only the crucial position of the 'new Germany' in the Euro-Atlantic structure but also the unavoidable tensions to which this gives rise. Many Germans might have wished to have been reunited without fuss and then left alone within the established structure: the process of unification, and the collapse of the broader order in central and eastern Europe, have demonstrated the unreality of such a hope. For the Germans, the choice ultimately might lie between the Atlantic and the European frameworks, but they have actually made a very brave try at reconciling them. At the same time as espousing political union and common foreign and security policy in the Community, they have instigated the development of the NACC as an attempt to sustain or extend the role of NATO, and they have paid much more than lip-service to the normative framework provided by the CSCE. The balancing act, though, has to be seen not only in the context of international pressures and priorities but also in the light of growing domestic tensions within the 'new Germany'. Along with other west European regimes, the Federal Republic has felt the strain of accommodating political and economic burdens at home and abroad; indeed, the German case shows the impossibility of separating the two domains, given the intense economic and social pressures resulting from the unification process itself. These tensions and pressures will play their own role in the future development of Atlantic relations.[16]

Yugoslavia and the new European states system

A predominant feature of the 1990s is the emergence of a new European states system; in the early 1990s at least, a central characteristic of this system was its lack of a settled structure and the fragility of many potential participants. In such a situation, the specific arrangements through which individual states come into membership of the system, and through which they carry out their responsibilities both to their populations and to the system, are highly significant.[17]

These general considerations have been given especially sharp and specific illustration in the early 1990s by the collapse of federal government in Yugoslavia and the emergence of actually or potentially warring states. In a poignant irony, the dangers of civil war in Yugoslavia had been a constant item on the agenda of cold-war planners in NATO for decades before it actually occurred; when it did occur, it was in a post-cold-war Europe in which the position of both superpowers was in question. The collapse of the USSR, and the uncertainty of American commitment, came together to aggravate an already unstable and potentially lethal situation. They have thus provided an acid test of the development of a specifically European framework for conflict resolution or containment, qualitatively different – at least until mid-1992 – from those posed by change elsewhere in eastern Europe.

When the threat of break-up in Yugoslavia first became apparent during 1990, it had to compete for attention with the dramatic developments not only in Europe more generally but also in the Gulf. Both the

United States and the Community at that stage were anxious that the conflict should be contained, and placed considerable weight on the continuation of a united Yugoslavia. Even when open fighting broke out in the spring of 1991, there was no urgency to either US or EC responses; when Douglas Hurd called for EC mediation in May 1991, it was seen as quite natural that this should be aimed at the preservation of the federation, and the subsequent EC mission took place within this context. Meanwhile, the Americans gave every indication of reluctance to get involved. It is important to note in this context that from the very earliest stage the USA and the Community rested their case substantially on the principles expressed in the CSCE: the protection of minority rights, the injunction against the changing of borders by force and the maintenance of legitimate governmental authorities. The problem was that hardly any of the parties in Yugoslavia itself subscribed to all of these dicta, and that many interpreted them according to their own preferences. Another perception in the American and Community positions was that neither of them had much in the way of leverage over the parties in Yugoslavia, although the Community had the economic weapon in the shape of existing and prospective trade arrangements.

The fundamental tension in the American and Community positions between order and change became a central theme of the developing crisis during 1991. Both the beginnings of EC mediation efforts and the June visit of James Baker to Belgrade took as their theme the need to keep the federation together. At this point, also, the use made of the CSCE principles could best be described as conservative – on the side of order rather than change in a situation of conflict. The Berlin meeting of the organization in June likewise set out an agenda for improving the crisis mechanism of the CSCE, at the same time as the US State Department was clearly coming down against secessionist movements, conscious of the possible analogy with the USSR. One conclusion from this phase of the crisis is that both the USA and the EC were placing order higher in their scale of priorities than change and the recognition of pluralism; another is that both were operating on false assumptions or wishful thinking about the possibility of limiting the Yugoslav conflict.[18]

By the autumn of 1991, two further features of the Yugoslav situation had become apparent. In the first place, the Americans seemed to have abdicated any responsibility for the safeguarding of order or the promotion of orderly change; the question was whether this constituted a designed line of policy or merely a passive acquiescence in events that were beyond Washington's control. Secondly, the Community's involvement had experienced a qualitative change, with the commitment of observers to safeguard a series of largely abortive ceasefires and the acceptance of what was in effect a mandate from the CSCE to promote an orderly resolution to the conflict. There is no doubt that some American officials saw the crisis as a European responsibility, and the EC as capable of acting where the CSCE and the USA alike were unable to do so. The Community, after all, had both a diplomatic mechanism and the economic leverage to affect events; the deployment of the observers, with Western European Union acting in the wings, seemed to bring together several elements of a new EC security presence.

The Community presence was not without its difficulties. Its members differed widely about the desirability of either holding Yugoslavia together or acceding to the independence requests of Slovenia and Croatia. Rapidly, Germany came to hold the key position in arguing for early recognition of the two breakaway republics, while Britain and France took the more conservative line. The peace conference set up by the Community under the chairmanship of Lord Carrington was severely handicapped by the tension between application of the CSCE principles and the reality of the conflict, which saw a degeneration into war fought by Serbia and the federal army against Croatia in particular. The bold declaration by Jacques Poos, the foreign minister of Luxembourg, in July, that 'this is the hour of Europe, not of America' began to appear a hostage to fortune, to say the least. But the Community did doggedly hold together; indeed, at times it appeared that this was the central aim of all EC policy.[19]

At the centre of the EC position was the contradiction between self-determination for the Slovenes and Croats and restoration of central control from Belgrade. More and more, it appeared that the political reality of the conflict demanded an orderly breakup of the Yugoslav federation, and this was the line that came to be associated above all with the Germans. In their case, domestic pressures combined with historical factors and the inclinations of individual policymakers to provide a powerful incentive for recognition, reinforced by developments on the ground as the federal army attacked Croatia. Difficult as it was to define and redefine the mission of the EC monitoring force, and at a later stage to decide on the scope of economic sanctions against the offending Serbs and their allies, the trend was clear: despite resistance from the British and the French, the Germans came increasingly to set the agenda, assisted by the fact that during the autumn of 1991 they chaired both the CSCE and WEU. The one institutional asset they did not possess was a seat on the Security Council of the United Nations; significantly, it was a French initiative that led during the autumn to UN involvement and the use of Cyrus Vance as a special representative. It was also France and Germany that first suggested the deployment of a UN force, after earlier French attempts to involve WEU on a large scale.

For the EC, though, the Yugoslav crisis continued to push at the limits of security collaboration, particularly in the light of negotiations within the intergovernmental conferences which were to lead to the Maastricht treaty. During the autumn and winter of 1991, the central point of tension was the increasingly assertive German support for recognition of Slovenia and Croatia, a thrust which was greeted with apprehension by the British and the French among others. At the same time, the status of the EC truce monitors in Croatia was an increasing cause for concern: the extension of their mandate beyond Slovenia put them directly in the firing line, and exposed them to attack by both sides in a confused yet violent conflict. By the time the EC-sponsored peace conference put forward a proposed new constitution for Yugoslavia in October, it was apparent that the Serbs were isolated in opposition, and also that the EC was under pressure to impose coercive measures against them. The German drive towards recognition combined with the move towards sanctions and the growing involvement of the UN to create a new direction and momentum for the conflict.

There are two possible alternative interpretations for the changes in the EC's relationship to the Yugoslav conflict during late 1991 and early 1992; significantly, both of them take as a central assumption continuing US abstention. On the one side, it can be argued that the Community was increasingly dominated by the German move to recognition – a move delayed only by the December agreement that Yugoslav republics should apply for the privilege. In this version, the ratcheting forward of EC policy, the involvement of the WEU as a military adviser, the eventual recognition of Slovenia and Croatia, and the partial cowing of Serbia are part of a process in which the Community became subverted, turned to the purposes of its dominant member with unpredictable consequences. On the other side, it is possible to construct a version of Community policies which sees them as the central component of a new convergence between a variety of multilateral institutions. The CSCE, WEU, and eventually the UN, were coopted by the EC in the cause of stabilization and a potential resolution of the conflict. Deployment of 14,000 UN peacekeeping troops during the spring of 1992 thus was the apotheosis of a new style of multilateral diplomacy, with the EC as the indispensable catalyst.

When the conflict took a new and dangerous turn in Bosnia-Herzegovina, during April 1992, the EC was again central to the process of crisis management, although by then the US was pursuing a new and much more assertive line. As the tragedy of the siege of Sarajevo became apparent during June and July, the limitations of the Community's role became equally obvious; the tendency was increasingly to look to the USA, to the UN or to national initiatives such as President Mitterrand's dramatic visit of early July, but the reluctance of all parties to grasp the nettle of military intervention was testimony to both the domestic and the international constraints still operating.

While the jury remains out on the long-term outcome of the Balkan crisis, particularly in the light of events in Bosnia-Herzegovina and possible escalation of the tensions in Kosovo, one thing is quite clear. The United States, whether by chance or design, for a long time played only a marginal role in the central parts of the unfolding drama, whereas the EC and its diplomacy were intimately – some have argued, almost too intimately – involved throughout. This is not to deny the contradictions and internal tensions in the Community posture, which were centred particularly on the competing claims of self-determination and the established order. The untidiness of the evolving policy, and the meaning it gained in the light of parallel debates about European political union, were integral to the process by which the conflict was contained; while the hopes and fears of many Europeans were bound up with the fate of Yugoslavia, the danger of intervention and escalation was averted, at least temporarily. By summer 1992, the Americans had first associated themselves firmly with the EC process and then with the UN action, but this still did not imply any kind of central or dominant role for them in what was essentially a European conflict. Significantly, the Americans' criticisms of the Community's role mounted as they experienced it at first hand, but there were no magic solutions to be had from Washington. At the same time, the expansion of activity on the part of the EC led to some uncomfortable frictions with the UN itself, as over the implementation of successive ceasefire agreements in Bosnia. It appeared that both the USA and the EC had at least temporarily come up against the limits of diplomatic 'carrying capacity', attempting not only to reconcile the demands of different negotiating processes but also to do this against the background of domestic uncertainties on both sides of the Atlantic.[20]

The Gulf conflict and its aftermath: maintaining the extra-European order

Whereas in the Yugoslav crisis the European Community played and is playing a central role, the same cannot be said for its collective presence in the Gulf crisis and war during 1990-91. 'Out-of-area' conflicts have been a problem for the Western alliance throughout its forty and more years, and the issues attending American leadership beyond the Atlantic arena have often been acute. Not only has there been a question mark against some aspects of American involvements and actions, from Vietnam to Grenada; there has also been a persistent centrifugal tendency among the Europeans as the demands of alliance have extended beyond the core theatre of central Europe. The Gulf crisis and Desert Storm presented many of the EC's members with questions they found either difficult or impossible to answer, and thus opened up long-standing issues in a new and demanding form. Its aftermath and the proclamation of a New World Order have only perpetuated some of the tensions.

When Saddam Hussein invaded and occupied Kuwait in August 1990, the situation presented a number of challenges and opportunities for the western allies. Some of the challenges were strategic: the threat to friendly regimes, to strategic resources and to transport routes. Others were less tangible but equally powerful: the threat to extinguish sovereignty, the use of force as an instrument of policy, the human rights aspects of the Iraqi occupation and pillaging, the environmental threat of large-scale pollution as the crisis wore on and broke into war. In a number of respects, though, the Iraqis presented an opportunity. The military position of the Iraqis and the nature of their aggression were uniquely conducive to the exercise of countervailing force and the mustering of a coalition in support of the Kuwaitis. From an American perspective, the moral balance was also heavily in favour of retaliation against the Baghdad regime, while at the same time the Americans alone had the capability to mount and sustain the scale of operation needed to halt and reverse the Iraqi actions.

This combination of factors greatly enhanced the ability of Washington to assemble and to maintain the broad-based coalition force which eventually ousted the Iraqis from Kuwait in spring 1991. It was clear from the start, though, that the participants in the coalition, not least the Europeans, approached the matter from diverse perspectives. In simple terms, the Americans certainly held the initiative and the high cards, but their ability to create commitment on the part of their allies was variable. While the British were the most eager of recruits to the cause, the French only persuaded themselves at a late stage to join the fray, and the Germans proved reticent about any form of military involvement or support. During the diplomatic build-up to the eventual conflict, the Europeans in the Community context were unable to produce a collective military position, although they were able to concert their diplomatic and economic measures in large part. Where the Community fell short, there was no shortage of condemnation from both the Americans and the British: the *Newsweek* headline 'Europe the Feeble' aptly illustrated the feeling among the Anglo-Saxons that a combination of deviousness, institutional shortcomings and plain funk had put paid to any standing held by the EC and its members as a group.[21]

American criticism of the Community was based on a number of palpable weaknesses in the EC position. Different members of the Community held radically different views on the feasibility and desirability of force. The Community process proved inadequate when faced with demands for immediate and large-scale assistance to the 'front-line states' in the Gulf region. Domestic constraints and preoccupations (for example, the impact of unification in the German case and by implication that of France) played a major role in distracting some Community members. Historical and other ties to some of the protagonists proved divisive at certain points, both in the diplomatic and in the military phase. Clearly, the Community as a collective entity did not perform spectacularly: the much-cited case of the Belgian refusal to supply ammunition to Britain came to stand as a symbol for the failure to go beyond diplomatic exhortation and declaration. More potent was the symbolism and the practical effect of NATO, in providing the basis of common tactical procedures and the capacity to fight an 'electronic battle' bringing together several forces and complex equipments.

The success of Desert Storm, and the apparent rout of the Iraqis, led to American expressions of triumphalism and the proclamation of a New World Order by the Bush administration, but much of 1991 and early 1992 seemed to provide evidence of the limitations of American leverage in the postwar phase. One thing the Americans could do was get their most prosperous allies to pay for many of the costs of the operation: the Germans and the Japanese contributed largely to the war chest, which for some meant the operation ran at a profit. Another thing they could achieve – but only up to a point – was the creation of a framework for broader Middle East negotiations. The diplomacy of James Baker enabled the Israelis and other regional actors, including Palestinians, to enter into talks which began at Madrid in the autumn of 1991. Much arm-twisting and calculated ambiguity was expended in the effort, but by the start of 1992 it was far from apparent where the talks were going. By the summer, it appeared that the most significant force for progress in the talks was the impetus for political change in Israel itself, with the defeat of the Shamir government in the June elections. While this accorded well with the preferences of the Washington administration, not least because of its electoral priorities, it was very unclear how far it expressed the impact of US policies themselves. The Bush administration also proclaimed the establishment of a new regime for arms sales in the region, which was supported by other western powers at the London summit in July 1991, and which was seen by some as the core of a new regional order to complement the broader world order. What they appeared unable to achieve through means short of renewed war was the downfall of Saddam Hussein himself; his persistence in the face of sanctions and threats, and his defiance of requirements for UN inspection of military facilities, put a question mark against the efficacy of the New World Order, which reached a point of high tension with the renewed threat of military action during July 1992. As in the Gulf war itself, it was the British and the Americans who took the central roles in the western response, albeit the British held the Presidency of the EC Council of Ministers at the time.

The Gulf crisis intersected with and came to be accompanied by a more widespread zone of conflict, running from the Mediterranean to the central Asian republics of the former Soviet Union. Even the seemingly contained operations of Desert Storm embroiled other actors, such as the Turks and the Iranians, not least through the travails of the Kurds, who saw a significant diplomatic and humanitarian input from the European Community countries. Indeed, it could be argued that the EC initiative in establishing safe havens for the Kurds was a proof immediately after the Gulf war that the mechanisms of Community foreign policy coordination were still in one piece. During 1991, though, the collapse of the Soviet Union threw open a host of often ancient questions affecting the Black Sea region, the Caucasus and the central Asian interior. The most severe – or savage – of these conflicts was that which set the Armenians against the Azerbaijanis, focused on the disputed enclave of Nagorno-Kharabakh. At this point, the seemingly separate domains of the 'NATO area' and the world beyond began to come into collision. By March 1992, the meetings of the NACC included both the Armenians and their rivals, while the remit of the CSCE had been extended to encompass the central Asian republics. There were also feedback effects into the more readily recognized NATO area, with increasing demands for membership from those in Europe who had so recently been part of the Soviet sphere. In none of these cases was there any clear indication either of the priority to be given to US leadership or of the ways in which US and EC initiatives might be coordinated.[22]

It is impossible here to do full justice to the complexities of the linkages arising from the appearance of this new 'arc of crisis'. Nor is it easy to identify its implications for the respective roles of the United States and the Community. Whereas in the Gulf context a series of factors had given effective dominance to the USA (it has been disputed by some whether this conferred legitimate leadership rights[23]), the eruption of the new conflicts seemed to occur in a kind of no man's land, where neither the United States nor the Community found it easy to establish a legitimate presence.[24] As we noted earlier, the differing capacities of the Americans and the Community both to pay attention and to exercise leverage were apparent in the security and the political domains: whereas the Americans could make their presence felt in the issue of nuclear proliferation, the Community had more say in the provision of humanitarian and economic assistance. Perhaps significantly, the CSCE and the NACC seemed to provide a relatively painless entrée into the diplomacy of the region and a way of accommodating new forces without unduly constraining them. From the point of view of Euro-Atlantic relations, this institutional diversity has strong links to the broader issue of 'variable geometry' for US/EC relations in the changing international political order.

Coping with the fall-out: migration, proliferation and pollution
The break-up of the Soviet Union and of its sphere of influence has created a number of pressing problems for western policymakers. Not least among them are those which could be described generically as 'fall-out': the human, military and social dangers emerging from the removal of the cap on nationalist conflicts, economic discontents and weapons proliferation. When the writ of Moscow ceased to run even in parts of Russia itself, it was inevitable that there would be leakages – of people, technology and pollutants – which would affect the comfortable societies of western Europe in particular. But these threats and risks are not solely a concern to the European Community: some of them relate directly to the imperatives of American policy in the absence of a 'partner' in the USSR, and to the search for a sustainable world order in the post-bipolar world.

For western Europe in general, the most material danger to ways of life and standards of living is that of voluntary or forced mass migration. This is not only a threat from the former Soviet bloc: the Community and its leaders are painfully aware of the pressure from the southern shores of the Mediterranean and further afield, especially on countries such as Germany with relatively liberal immigration regimes. During 1992, the growing wave of displaced persons associated with the Yugoslav conflict created further pressures and at times a hint of panic among west European policymakers, reflecting a series of major dilemmas. With domestic calls for more restrictive practices, particularly in France and Germany, and ever greater pressures from outside, there are few ready policy solutions. One tactic has been to proffer aid to countries of origin on the simple basis that if things get better at home fewer refugees or economic migrants will be forced west or north. Another line of policy uses the EC itself as a cover, with the aim of producing effective restrictions on entry to the Community as a whole, while avoiding the opprobrium of being seen to favour new limitations. In both respects, the German position is pivotal: it is only Germany that has the magnetic effect on potential migrants, the relatively open door and the means to deliver effective economic rewards for restraint. While the pressure on countries such as Italy increased markedly in the wake of the Yugoslav conflict, it is still the Germans who hold many of the keys to progress.[25]

The mass movement of peoples is to all intents and purposes a European issue resolvable only by Europeans. Although the Americans can state the general case for freedom of movement, they are in no position materially to affect the situation, nor are they without their own problems in terms of relations with Central and South America. There is, though, a further tension in the American position as it relates to what might broadly be described as European society. At many points in the unfolding of the east European drama, American voices have called upon the Community not to close off the possibility of improvement in the economic and political lot of the 'outsiders'. Thus, there was pressure from Washington for rapid progress towards 'Europe Agreements' between the Community and Poland, Hungary and Czechoslovakia during 1990 and 1991. At the same time, there has been an assumption that the EC will take the strain of economic and other forms of assistance, while in the USA itself the Congress has exerted continual pressure for spending restraint. The domestic imperatives facing administrations on both sides of the Atlantic do not permit policymakers to ignore the financial and human costs of liberal postures, and the natural inclination is to play to the loudest elements of the domestic audience.

Alongside the dangers posed by mass unplanned movements of people has gone that of the uncontrolled diffusion of military technology and assets. There are a number of aspects to this issue, in particular the distinction between attempts to control the proliferation of weapons or technologies and the parallel efforts to reach arms control agreements at the level of the US and Russian governments. Whereas the old-style non-proliferation regime was essentially a superpower domain, in keeping with the American and Soviet control of weapons and technologies, the disappearance of one half of the balance has led to major fears of instability. The estimated 30,000 nuclear warheads in the Commonwealth of Independent States, 12,000 of them relatively mobile tactical weapons, constitute a major threat to military equilibrium if they are not effectively controlled; disputes even between the two major actors in the CIS – Russia and Ukraine – have generated fears that the nuclear balance will become both more complex and more unstable. This is far from being solely an American concern: the British and the French, as established nuclear powers, and the Germans along with others as potential targets, have a clear interest in the issue, but they do not have the weight or the expertise to tip the balance decisively for or against proliferation. The Americans have both, to such an extent that they can provide practical services to those wishing to dismantle nuclear forces and convincingly identify those who wish to proliferate illegally. This leverage is not always effective, however, where the established state authorities are in no position to implement agreements solemnly concluded; the American agitation about the arms control consequences of the Soviet break-up in late 1991 and 1992 gave powerful evidence of this difficulty. Although it appeared that the sweeping arms control agreements of June 1992 had created a new momentum, the fear that Russian governments might be unwilling or unable to implement the reductions persists.[26]

The Americans are also the guardians of the arms control regime in a more general sense. As the most experienced and the most potent arms control and arms reduction negotiators available, they naturally take precedence in the handling of the post-Soviet renegotiation. One of the problems they face in this respect is that of finding negotiating partners who can make their agreements stick, and American anxiety on this count has been apparent at each stage of the Soviet break-up. Moreover, their very strength is at times a weakness or a limitation: some of the most pressing arms control needs are not those of nuclear proliferation or strategic arms reduction but those surrounding the uncontrolled dispersion of conventional weapons. In this domain, the Americans are important but not always crucial. More significant may be parts of the multilateral arms control and security regime erected around the CSCE, including the CFE agreement of December 1990 which was approaching final ratification and entry into force during the summer of 1992. In this connection also, the European Community has an established status denied it in the field of nuclear weapons. Its long-standing collective presence in the CSCE, and the new tasks accorded it through the Maastricht treaty in the field of foreign and security policy, provide a basis for development of new and far-reaching policy initiatives. Indeed, the association of the WEU with the Community in this context gives an expanded role to nuclear non-proliferation and other arms control measures on the Community agenda. There is, though, cause to question the capacity of the Community to develop quickly enough or in a unified manner, and thus be able to supplant the still dominant role of the United States, founded on its military and technological status.

The break-up of the Soviet Union and the Soviet bloc is not merely a question of political and economic destabilization. At the centre of many concerns in Europe has been the potential for a different kind of fall-out: the spreading of environmental degradation and the expense entailed in containing or reversing it. At the moment, the handling of this issue is in a sense bifurcated. The global level of action saw the 'Earth summit' in Rio during the summer of 1992 as a prime focus, with the stress on broad-ranging standards to meet challenges such as global warming. At the summit, the USA occupied the role of villain, not least because of the Bush administration's preoccupation with the domestic audience in an election year; at several points, there was conflict with the position of the Community, although it cannot be pretended that the EC was at all clear about its priorities or its commitments.[27]

The adage 'act locally, think globally' hits home especially hard in the new Europe. Here, the catastrophic results of forty years of forced and heedless industrialization within the former Soviet bloc have a very immediate impact, and the Community has a major role, carried further in the Maastricht treaty. Such challenges as the making safe of nuclear power sites, the decontamination of whole regions and the civilizing of entire industries are costly and demanding, and likely to claim an increasing part of European attention in the 1990s.[28] Are they, though, a proper subject for transatlantic coordination or action? The likely competition between providers in the new environmental protection industries may well ensure that there are transatlantic tensions in this area, but ultimately it could be argued that the European environment is a security matter for the Europeans, especially where it comes into linkage with the other aspects of 'fall-out' identified here: the movements of populations and the diffusion of nuclear danger.

Building a new institutional framework

The pattern of international and European institutions built up during the cold war came under increasing strain in the late 1980s as the 'freeze' imposed by the division of Europe gradually gave way to a new turbulence. It would be misleading, though, to imply that the new institutional pluralism of the late 1980s and 1990s is a sudden development: most of its components have been around for a long time, dating not only from the origins of the cold war itself but also from previous periods of detente, and reflecting the gradual leakage of political and security affairs away from the straitjacket of NATO and the Warsaw Pact. By 1989, the use of an increasing range of institutional channels for the expression of diverse interests, and the diffusion of political and security risks or costs, had become an established part of the European landscape. Within this landscape, the continuing role and relevance of NATO, and the ability of the European Community to take up new burdens, were a central cause for concern and debate.

The first set of developments to dominate, after the break-up of the east European stalemate in 1989 and 1990, concerned NATO. As the centrepiece of the Western alliance, the organization had been defined not only by the organic link between the United States and European security but also by the persistence of a seemingly monolithic threat from the East. It had also experienced a continuing tension between the demands of defence and the promises of detente – between a primarily military conception of alliance and the broader implications of political coalition-building in the security arena. This tension had been expressed as far back as the late 1960s with the Harmel Report, but it was the changing situation in Germany and the Warsaw Pact that brought it bubbling to the surface again during 1990. The question was not merely one of coping with the disappearance of the seemingly permanent threat: it encompassed the position and role of the 'new Germany' and the 'new United States', and it centred particularly on the need for the continued denuclearization of Europe.

During 1990, the response at the institutional level was twofold. On the one hand there was an intense search for a new doctrine at the military and the political level, capable of resolving or at least containing the new tensions while retaining the umbilical link between the USA and Europe. The first fruits of this were seen in the London Declaration of June 1990, which very firmly made the case for a shift of emphasis towards the political in NATO's activities, and for the use of the organization as a bridge not only between the USA and Europe but also between the two halves of a newly undivided Europe itself. On the other hand, the Declaration also restated the character of NATO as a 'nuclear alliance' by emphasizing the need for appropriate maintenance of nuclear forces in Europe.[29] At this point, the alliance looked as if it could manage to bring off a complex balancing act, and this appeared to be confirmed by the process of German unification. Not only was the need for the alliance reconfirmed, but the new German state was firmly included in it.

The process since mid-1990, though, has cast some doubt on this achievement. In the first place, the dynamics of the accelerating 'disarmament race' between the United States, the Soviet Union and the Commonwealth of Independent States have transformed the nuclear environment for NATO. The agreements reached at the Bush/Yeltsin summit of June 1992, which promised an elimination of Russia's land-based intercontinental missiles and reductions of both American and Russian arsenals to one-third of the existing levels, was the culmination of a series of events which would have been unthinkable as late as 1990. It appears realistic to assume that in the foreseeable future there will be an effective denuclearization of Europe through the removal of American tactical weapons, while the consequences of the 'peace dividend' debate in the USA will lead inexorably to a draw-down of American forces in Europe to produce a level of less than a third of the pre-1989 figure. Ironically, the effectiveness of allied cooperation in the Gulf war served only to conceal the fact that it continued the process of American disengagement from the European theatre. It should not be assumed that NATO will cease effectively to be a nuclear alliance or that it will dissolve as the Americans retreat. What it may well mean is that the alliance will resemble increasingly the notion of the North Atlantic Treaty as a guarantee which can be exercised at arm's length.

This, though, ignores the decided American interest in retaining security and political influence in the European theatre. One of the dominant trends in the NATO of 1990-92 has been the attempt to create a new context both for the continued engagement of the USA and for the inclusion of the new east European democracies. The implication is that while the military core of NATO will shrink (and indeed already has shrunk considerably), the political existence of the alliance will be refurbished and form the core of a political/security coalition. The centrepiece of this process is likely to be the new North Atlantic Cooperation Council, associating the eastern states, including those of the Caucasus and central Asia, with the alliance's new political aims. By exploiting this aspect of the alliance, its supporters hope to build out from the continuing military core to facilitate the process of 'civilianization' and military reductions in eastern Europe and the CIS. The Copenhagen and Rome NATO Council meetings during 1991 thus represented in some ways a sea-change in the organization and the distinctive alliance contribution to a new institutional architecture – the essential accompaniment to the development of a new European Community identity in the security field.[30] This impression was strengthened by the Oslo ministerial meeting of July 1992, during which an explicit division of labour between NATO, WEU and the Community in the peacekeeping field was canvassed.

The picture is by no means as clear as this implies, since the emerging EC identity is itself not only a focus of debate but also a function of the NATO and broader Atlantic evolution. Although it can be seen as a rather stagey piece of public diplomacy, the demand from President Bush at the NATO Rome summit in December 1991 that the Europeans should tell the USA whether they still wanted it expresses a genuine uncertainty. Importantly, the debate about the new mission of NATO during 1990 and 1991 intersected at many points with the developing views of Europeans about a common foreign and security policy for the Community. The Dublin summit of May 1990 saw the bringing together of the existing thrust for economic and monetary union with the new realities of German unification and east European break-up to create a new dynamic in the Community centred on the move to political union. A key question in this process was the relationship of the EC institutions and processes with NATO and the more explicitly military aspects of security. As NATO moved to try to create a new political role, the Community was moving to go beyond the 'political and economic aspects of security' which had been stressed in the Single European Act.

The result of this implicit dialogue between the alliance and the Community has been a form of dynamic tension, which is still unresolved. The Community process during 1991 came to focus particularly upon the tensions between the 'Atlanticist' and the 'European' ideas: the one was represented particularly by the British, with their continued emphasis on the need for a strong transatlantic connection; the other, by the French, with their push for a strong European identity and tangible measures of military cooperation. Both tendencies focused institutionally upon the role of Western European Union, and also upon the position of Germany. WEU provided an institutional solution-in-waiting for both the Atlanticist and the European tendencies, representing as it did not only the potential European pillar of a new Atlantic alliance but also the potential centrepiece of a European defence policy. Things came out into the open as the Maastricht conference approached, with the Anglo-Italian proposal and the French-German-Spanish response of October 1991. The first of these placed WEU firmly into a NATO context, but also contained significant moves towards a strong European pillar with its own priorities and identity. The second, while stressing the need for concrete moves towards specifically European cooperation such as a French-German (and by implication European) army corps, stressed the continuing need for an organic Atlantic connection.

The Maastricht provisions on political union constituted an institutional compromise which can be claimed as a victory by both the Atlanticist and the European tendencies. By its careful highlighting of the NATO link, it gave the Atlanticists what they wanted; but, by its promise of review and reformulation, it left open the development of much more substantial European institutions. WEU was presented as an organic part of the EC process, but at the same time as the European pillar of the alliance. Meanwhile, events moved on: the pressure for WEU coordination of EC military operations in Yugoslavia that was felt in the autumn of 1991 was later defused by the use of the UN, but during the summer of 1992 WEU again emerged as the institutional solution to the issues raised by enforcement of sanctions against Serbia and Montenegro. At the same time, the Helsinki CSCE meeting and the Oslo NATO summit of June 1992 elaborated further the notion of functional links between the political and the military arms of the future new European order. The drive for concrete European collaboration on a series of security problems such as those relating to non-proliferation and arms sales likewise gives the EC and WEU a central focus in the implementation of the New World Order in Europe and beyond, but the continuing uncertainty about the nature of the order which is to be preserved does not provide a firm foundation for considered institutional development.[31]

Alongside the Euro-Atlantic dynamic of the relationship between NATO, WEU and the EC has gone the further elaboration of the CSCE framework. Indeed, there are arguments which would suggest that CSCE in its various manifestations is the central institutional force in the 'new Europe' or the new Euro-Atlantic system. It has taken a central role in shaping the transition in eastern Europe, and in establishing a normative framework for the consideration of what are essentially post-imperial questions both there and in the CIS. The Americans have come strongly to favour the CSCE method for expressing the new European reality, not least perhaps because the CSCE gives them and the Canadians a continuing institutional engagement in the affairs of the changing continent. Not only this, but the elasticity of the CSCE framework can see it extending to the Caucasus and central Asia in dealing with the break-up of the Soviet Union. When combined with the NACC, which has at least the potential to handle the military transition, it can be argued that the CSCE matches the needs for adaptation and flexibility within an accepted normative and quasi-legal order.[32]

But the CSCE is in many ways institutionally limited. Indeed, that is one of its strengths: it represents the full range of states and regimes, it operates on consensus, it has no capacity to translate moral and political injunctions into military action. As revealed in the Yugoslav conflict, it can highlight the issues but it cannot give them tangible institutional expression. The escalation of the Bosnian conflict during 1992 demonstrated not only the ways in which the CSCE might provide a forum for debate and act as a facilitator of common action, but also the need for other institutions such as NATO or WEU when it comes to concerted action, for example the enforcement of sanctions or the provision of humanitarian aid. When the CSCE attempted to initiate an observer mission to monitor the Armenian/Azerbaijani conflict over Nagorno-Kharabakh, the failure of the warring parties to agree was an insurmountable stumbling-block.[33]

As a result, the attempt to institutionalize a new European order has come to reflect the extension of 'variable geometry' on a grand scale. Originally coined to reflect the interaction of governments and institutions in the EC, this expression has come to mean a lot more in the context of a changing Europe (and western Asia). While the United States has come to support a CSCE/NACC regime in fairly explicit terms, the development of an explicit CSCE/European Community institutional interaction has been apparent as well, and there is clearly also a role for a CSCE/EC/UN role in some cases. During 1991, this was elaborated particularly in the case of Yugoslavia, but there were signs also that the remedy might be applied in such areas as the Armenian/Azerbaijani conflict or other intra-CIS problems, with appropriate help from NATO and the WEU. As if this exercise of 'variable geometry' were not enough, the intimate relationship between economic assistance and the security issue brought such bodies as the IMF and the European Bank for Reconstruction and Development also into play. By July 1992, the intervention of the G7 alongside the existing involvement of a series of European or Euro-Atlantic bodies had produced what the optimists might see as an interlocking cluster of institutional actions. Others might have characterized the situation as gridlock rather than interlock.

Does this mean that the European arena now suffers from a severe case of 'institutional overcrowding', in which there is a case for the elimination of some of the overlapping and potentially competing institutions?[34] One conclusion is certainly clear: we have moved a long way from the situation in which the Atlantic alliance (and the Warsaw Pact) could act as the exclusive institutional expression of relations between the superpowers and their European partners or clients. There are clearly also problems which emerge not just from inter-institutional frictions but also from the ways in which these are infused with national or sectional interests; the position of the French or the British in this respect expresses not only their institutional preferences or their vision of 'Europe' but also their relationships with both the Germans and the Americans and their perceptions of interest in regional issues in Europe and beyond. The American position in turn is conditioned not by institutional logic as much as by the anxiety to preserve a residual voice in Europe and the political leverage which goes with it, while at the same time responding to budgetary and domestic political pressures. For other major participants in this complex square-dance, much the same kind of mixed motives could be identified.

The net result is that the development of a new institutional architecture for the Euro-Atlantic community has thus far been a reflection of adhocery, political expediency and the force of circumstances. In many instances, it has not represented the working out of a conscious logic or design so much as the interaction of national and institutional interests within the constraints set by domestic political expediency or the pressure of international crisis. That does not mean that it is ineffective: rather, it means that it does not yet encapsulate a new (or renewed) consensus on the institutional framework within which the changing European and world orders might be nourished. As noted earlier in this book, the achievement or the recognition of such a consensus will depend on the working through of economic and political forces at many levels and on both sides of the Atlantic.

Conclusion

In this chapter, the focus has been primarily upon the ways in which the US and the EC, individually and collectively, have responded to the political challenges of the 1990s. These challenges are more complex, more mercurial and less predictable than those of the cold-war era, and they demand innovative and imaginative responses on a number of levels. The creation of order in a new European states system, embedded within a more turbulent global context and penetrated by new economic and social forces, is one of the central challenges to the notion of a Euro-Atlantic partnership. By the middle of 1992, the clearest feature of the situation was its lack of clarity and definition: the continuing landslide of change in the former Soviet bloc had perhaps slowed, but it was uncertain whether it might not recommence in the light of events in Czechoslovakia and the CIS. In the former Yugoslavia, the limits of diplomacy and ad-hoc institutional engagement appeared to have been reached, while in the Middle East and surrounding areas the pressures of US electoral politics appeared to play a major role. The escalating refugee crisis in Europe not only pushed all other stories off the front page, but revealed the fault lines between Europeans as much as between the USA and Europe more generally. The argument here has identified not only these and other specific challenges to European Community/United States partnership, in and around the 'new Europe', but also some underlying issues which must be resolved if US/EC relations are to contribute effectively to the new order:

– First, there is the issue of the American presence and the American role. How will Americans themselves conceive of their continuing entanglement with a more turbulent Europe, at a time of considerable domestic challenge and tension? How will Europeans, both within and outside the EC, perceive the costs and benefits of a continued and perhaps restructured US presence in European politics and institutions? The evidence from the cases and issues explored here is at best inconclusive, and in many instances contradictory, with assertiveness accompanying abstention and European suspicions running alongside a strong drive to keep Washington interested.
– Second, there is the question of European autonomy and the capacity of the Community to express it. There is little doubt that the demand and the opportunity for European self-assertiveness exists, but this serves merely to underline the limitations of the Community as an expression of a European identity. The continuing ambivalence of

many Community members about not only its internal workings but also its international presence and role feeds directly into European/ American relations, and is a central factor in any attempt to define a new partnership. As we have noted, there is very often a desire on the part of others for Community involvement which outruns or miscalculates the EC's real capacity to act. 'Others' in this context can be taken to include those Americans who argue strongly that the Community should be playing a more appropriate, and by implication more assertive, role.

- Third, there is the question of interests and priorities. In all of the cases examined here, it has been evident not only that American and Community interests can come into collision, but also that the identification of priorities by either Americans or Community members is subject to a host of pressures and often conflicting perceptions. In dealing with the great problems of a changing political order, Americans and Europeans may agree or disagree across the Atlantic, but they can agree and disagree also across the Channel, the Rhine, the Pyrenees, the Rockies or Pennsylvania Avenue. The shaping of such agreements and disagreements contains not only political elements, but economic calculations and constraints, especially in the light of increasing economic interpenetration.

- Finally, there is the issue of institutions, which is a matter both of formal structure and of symbolism and political commitment. The institutional landscape of the new Europe is crowded and its boundaries ill-defined. There can be no doubt that in any institutional developments the US and the EC will be crucial factors, but will this be for positive or negative reasons? A new institutional structure will need to be agile and adaptive, but it will also need to express a consensus – not at present apparent – on principles of policy. The cases discussed above indicate that the institutional solution to any one European problem is simultaneously likely to be complex and unlikely to apply to any other such problem.

These assessments reflect not only the untidiness and fluidity of the political context for Euro-Atlantic partnership, but also the ways in which it interacts with the domestic concerns of the US and the EC and the developing global economy. Chapter 5 will attempt to synthesize both our conclusions and some possible future scenarios for development in US/EC relations.

5
CONCLUSIONS

Chapter 1 identified a number of areas in which EC/US relations faced changes that are radical and structural in nature, rather than marginal or conjunctural. It argued further that there has been a cognitive shift in the perceptions of policymakers and elites as well as a substantive change in the context in which they operate. A crucial characteristic of this process of change is that it has accentuated linkages between economic and security issues and between domestic and international pressures. In so doing, it has considerably complicated policy formulation and, still more, policy implementation. In these circumstances, the identification and pursuit of common interests is both desirable and challenging. Even the choice of procedures or institutional mechanisms for collaboration has itself become a matter for political debate. Chapters 2–4 assessed the validity of this argument by looking at how the EC and the US are responding to the challenges of 'domestic' identity and governance, the management of the global economy and the search for political order in Europe and the world beyond.

The conclusions to be presented in this chapter fall into three areas:

(1) There is an assessment, on the basis of the evidence from Chapters 2–4, of the initial assumptions and arguments. It is argued that change poses two central problems for Euro-Atlantic relations. On the one hand, there is *the differential impact of change* across the issue areas explored; on the other, there is a *challenge to governance* on both sides of the Atlantic, arising from the increased linkages between domestic political and economic uncertainties and international change.

99

(2) The possible future for Euro-Atlantic relations is considered, and an effort is made to identify the direction in which events are moving. We conclude that the most likely future for Euro-Atlantic relations is one of *competitive cooperation*, in which collaboration and competition will run in parallel and create both challenges and opportunities for policymakers.

(3) Finally, the chapter suggests how Euro-Atlantic relations should be conducted, given the way in which conditions in the 1990s are likely to unfold. We argue that Euro-Atlantic relations must focus on how the US and the EC can establish a stable framework within which competition can take place and enhance the coordination of US and EC efforts to maintain a stable political order. The focus, it is argued, should not be on efforts to reaffirm or rebuild *the Atlantic relationship*, whether by a new treaty to follow on from the 1990 Atlantic Declaration or by some other means. This approach might be called a 'results-based' or 'aspirational' approach. Rather, it should be on how to enhance the ability of the US and the EC to make mutually supportive contributions to maintaining a stable economic and political order. This might be called a process approach. Such an approach is likely to require more than pragmatism. It will require innovative approaches to dealing with interdependence, which could usefully form part of a US/EC treaty or agreement.

One further conclusion should be made crystal clear at this juncture. In Chapter 1, we posed the question of whether the Euro-Atlantic relationship is a good investment for the 1990s. This study sets out some of the reasons why this question is posed. It also argues that it is worth investing resources and energy not so much in order to maintain a special Euro-Atlantic relationship, but in order to build a stable economic and political order. This requires continued investment in US/EC cooperation and even in efforts to promote what is effectively transatlantic integration.

The challenge

In assessing the ways in which change has impacted upon Euro-Atlantic relations, one is concerned both with the incidence of change and with the ways in which it is recognized by policymakers and reflected in their actions. Chapters 2-4 explored three areas of change: the domestic politics and economics of the USA and the EC, the management of the world economy, and the search for political order in a turbulent world. One important conclusion from this analysis is that the incidence and pace of change in each of the three areas varies. Whereas the issue of domestic governance responds to such forces as shifts in the electoral cycle, structural changes in the world economy take place over decades. In the case of changes in political or security issues, the pace of events and the incidence of crisis during the 1990s pose problems that are different again. Although crisis situations are generally of a short-term nature, the merging of economic and security relations means that the US and EC responses to them are still linked to long-term structural factors involving further complexities.

Thus, in dealing with the questions raised by the collapse of the USSR, both the USA and the Community have had to face a more complex, interdependent and interlinked world. Among the factors involved at any one time are: the salience of domestic pressures for intervention or abstention; the financial costs of policy or, more accurately, the ability of policymakers to persuade domestic constituencies that security gains are worth short-term economic costs; the possibilities of action through channels such as the IMF or EBRD; and the priority accorded to questions such as nuclear proliferation or even the preservation of particular regimes in the former Soviet sphere. But these factors cannot be divorced from the longer-term question of the role of the USA and the EC in the world economy or the international political order. There is, in short, a central issue for policymakers: that of identifying, evaluating and responding to change in three different dimensions and above all of coping with the complex linkages between the dimensions.

Domestic governance

In this dimension the central question is quite simply, can the EC and American sides of the partnership cope with the challenge of governance in the 1990s? Not so long ago, this question would have appeared otiose, with the USA celebrating the triumph of democracy over communism and the Community responding to the political revolutions in Europe in 1989–91 by preparing to take a qualitative step towards European Union in Maastricht. The evidence presented in Chapter 2, however, suggests that the celebrations have produced the inevitable hangover and recriminations about who is to pick up the bill.

The Community post-Maastricht appears to be facing not the triumph of a new form of governance but the resurgence of some rather old and thought-to-be superseded habits. Whatever the fate of the treaties

themselves, the capacity of the Community to move beyond intergovern-
mentalism has been challenged, not only by the Danes and others through
formal political processes, but also by the continuing narrowing of
horizons arising from recession and doubts about the democratic legitimacy of decisionmaking within the EC. The mood of Community institutions is defensive, and that of member governments hesitant. Neither can
the pressures from the outside world be ignored which call for a greater,
more coherent role for the EC, certainly in international economic questions but increasingly in political and security ones as well, but each looks
over its shoulder at the more hostile domestic forces gathered there. In
trade the world looks expectantly to the EC to support multilateralism,
but this is not an easy idea to sell to European farmers. In financial and
monetary relations the recession of the early 1990s has driven home the
vulnerability of individual European countries to external pressures and
has raised doubts about whether there is the political will to move
towards a single currency. In security questions the horrors of the Yugoslav civil war and 'ethnic cleansing' have challenged the ability of the
Community and its members to go beyond declaratory diplomacy and
economic sanctions. But this does not mean that the longer-term process
of integration has come to a halt, or that the Community will not continue
to grow in importance. But it does mean that policymakers in the USA
and elsewhere will need to distinguish between the often bitter internal
Community debate or short-term setbacks and the underlying significance of the Community's evolution.

In the United States, the main expression of doubt about the effectiveness of government is the apparent inability to address major domestic
problems such as the persistent budget deficit, the decline in educational
standards and the progressive alienation of sections of society, as illustrated most dramatically by the Los Angeles riots of spring 1992. The
Democrat-controlled Congress invariably seeks to focus political debate
on such issues in the run-up to an election. But the difference between
1991-2 and 1987-8 is the degree to which the 'USA-first' theme has
found a resonance throughout the country and has been shared by conservative republicans and liberal democrats alike. At the heart of the
debate about governance in the USA is taxation, which is itself a proxy
for the role of the state in providing, for example, health, education and
infrastructure. In domestic issues, just as in transatlantic relations, the end
of the cold war might well have removed for the administration by the
constraints on internal dissent, including debate about the redistributive
function of the state. For forty years, the imperative to provide for

external security against the threat of Soviet communism has been a given in US politics. The removal of the security blanket will make it easier to fan the embers of the debate on national wealth redistribution, which have smouldered but never ignited into political conflict. Not agreeing on how to reduce the budget deficit has merely been a means of postponing such discussion. A further major and possibly growing question for governance in the US is what to assign to the competence of the state and what to federal competence. This is an important question when the US federal government finds itself unable to conclude international agreements on trade and investment issues, for example, because it is afraid of trampling on state competence. The result of such pressures is a governmental preoccupation with domestic issues which threatens to limit the USA's ability to operate effectively on the international stage, whether in the Middle East or in the GATT.

This, possibly inevitable, reorientation towards domestic and away from foreign policy concerns was reflected in the July 1992 appointment of James Baker as George Bush's campaign manager. From being the last best hope of American diplomacy, he now became the last best hope of Bush's re-election – in the face of an opponent, it must be added, whose convention address notoriously assigned only 141 words to foreign policy. In trade policy, promises to Midwestern farmers to provide subsidies undermined a long-standing US policy of commitment to reducing or even eliminating farm subsidies. If US farmers are important voters, so are those in France. In monetary policy, a return to benign neglect, or even talking down the dollar, was in line with a desire to see a US economic revival, but it exacerbated tensions within the EMS and provides a rather negative example for the Europeans. If Maastricht is ratified, the EC will merely be following the US example if it bases monetary policy on internal needs at the expense of its trading partners. This did not prevent the US Federal Reserve from criticizing the German Bundesbank for pursuing deflationary monetary policies. The imperatives of engagement in the Gulf, the Balkans or the CIS might be strident, but policy was determined as much by electoral considerations as by the role of the US in the New World Order. As in the case of the Community, short-term factors seem temporarily to have obscured more benign longer-term objectives; but these short-term political responses also demonstrate how greatly the American domestic debate has been affected by long-standing structural factors which limit the USA's ability to influence international events.

In these conditions, the question 'But can they cope?' is far from redundant. It goes to the heart of the issue of governance, which is in its turn about effective transatlantic cooperation in the 1990s. If the authorities in the US and the Community – in whatever guises they may appear – have insufficient time, authority or attention to give to such cooperation, then the chances of each party developing separately are that much greater. It is even more serious if their distractedness goes beyond the politics of elections or of referenda, and represents a long-term trend towards introversion or isolationism in the face of international challenge. There is more than ever a need for coordination because of the centrality of the combined forces of the US and EC in the international economic and political orders. Neither the US nor the EC can resolve the increasingly complex challenges of international order alone. At the same time either could inflict considerable damage on the other and on the international system if it rejected cooperation in favour of the pursuit of its own interests. This is the challenge of the future, on both sides of the ocean.

Roles in the economic and political orders

Given the growing market and policy interdependence between the USA and the EC, how each deals with the challenge of domestic governance is the key to understanding their responses to the challenge of changes in the international economic and political order. In the economic sphere, there are well-established institutions and channels for handling major issues, such as the GATT and various financial bodies, but even so policy integration has not kept up with increasing interdependence. As a result, systemic differences between the EC, the US and other major trading partners, notably Japan, have come to the fore. Domestic preoccupations of both the US and the EC have meant that neither has been able to frame positive or rapid responses to external challenges. In the case of the Community, this expresses itself in difficulties in reaching a common position among the Twelve. In the case of the USA, coming up with initiatives is no problem, but getting the agreement of domestic constituencies or Congress is another matter altogether. As noted in Chapter 3, this raises important questions about the future of the US commitment to multilateralism.

The search for political order, and the connected politics of security in Europe and elsewhere, raise very different problems for Euro-Atlantic cooperation. As Chapter 4 indicated, the central difficulty is not only an absence of agreed rules but also uncertainties about which institutional channel of action to use (NATO, WEU, the EC, the CSCE, the UN, etc.). The US and the EC have responded to the transformed world in very different ways, but both have had to grapple with the turbulence created by the overthrow of existing national authorities in the former Soviet bloc, and the absence of legitimated replacements. Although the USA, by virtue of its superpower status, might be assumed to have the right of precedence in an area that touches on crucial (nuclear) security issues, geopolitical proximity and the increased importance of economic issues in European security has given the EC a prominence that it does not always welcome. The impact of post-cold-war politics has led to a similar hesitancy in the USA. One possible response, alongside the 'domestic obsession', might be a resort to bilateral dealings or 'special relationships' between the USA and other major actors. For western Europe, this would inevitably mean Germany, both in the economic and (less certainly) in the political sphere. But Chapters 3 and 4, and the evidence to hand in mid-1992, seem to indicate that uncertainty over the German role in both the economic and the political orders will be a continuing theme of developments in Europe as well as in US/EC relations. Although the weight of the Community's dominant member is in many respects as influential as that of the EC acting collectively, German ambivalence poses a major challenge to the management of transatlantic relations.

The challenge of the future
In short, both the USA and the EC face problems not only in redefining or establishing an identity or a role for themselves, but also in responding to the varying pace of change in the domestic, the international economic and the political arenas. Against this background, and remembering that one must start from where we are rather than from where the policy community might like to be, three possible scenarios for the future Euro-Atlantic relationship appear plausible, but none is without its problems.

First, there could be a greater degree of transatlantic policy *integration* to match the integration of economies that the markets have already brought about. In the field of trade and investment policy, there would certainly seem to be a clear need for this. The alternative of retaining the status quo seems unlikely to be stable and could easily slip into disintegration as either side uses systemic differences as grounds for constructing defensive regional blocs. But how should such integration be brought about? In previous periods a US hegemony obliged others to follow the US model or rules of the game. But the EC is no longer ready to accept this. Nor, for that matter, is the US ready to follow the EC model for dealing with international interdependence. A harmonization of policies seems equally unlikely given the quite important systemic differences that continue to divide the two sides. In short, the EC and the US represent competing systems of rules. Increased interdependence heightens the tensions by making more and more domestic issues the subject of international negotiations. This not only increases the scope for conflict between the two; it also means that harmonization becomes increasingly difficult. We are faced with a world in which the USA and the Community will continue to be intimately interconnected but incompletely integrated. Apart from the practical difficulties of such transatlantic policy integration, there is the question of whether it is desirable, given the responsibilities of each side to support a multilateral trading system.

A second possible scenario could be described as *separate development* or disengagement. This would emphasize one aspect of developments during the 1980s and 1990s: domestic preoccupations and the drift towards economic bloc-building. As discussed in Chapter 3, the pressures of 'expansive regionalism' in Europe, which were centred on the EC, and the moves towards NAFTA in the Americas, lend weight to this possibility. Divergent views of security interests and obligations might also reinforce the tendency. In principle, it might be argued, there is nothing to prevent an explicit division of the responsibilities (or burden) of maintaining economic and political order. But this scenario underestimates the impact of interdependence and the EC's current (and, in the medium term, probably continuing) deficiencies in effective international political action. It also has to rely on heroic assumptions about the capacity or inclination of the 'bloc builders' to recognize the need and to conclude effective agreements on the division of labour, if mutual antagonism is to be avoided. As noted in Chapter 1, the calculation of the costs of burden-sharing in the transformed world of the 1990s is complex. Given the domestic constraints and the complexity of the linkages, the task of maintaining stable US/EC relations seems certain to exceed the capacities of those who have to administer policies. As noted above, a retreat to bilaterism and 'special relationships' might result, but this scenario ignores both the complex networks of interdependence and the ambivalence at the centre of German policy.

The third – and most likely – scenario is one of *competitive cooperation*. The phrase encapsulates the ways in which domestic developments claim the attention of policymakers in both the Community and the USA, and the ways in which this feeds through into international competition.

As has been argued at several points, this competition is felt through the mutual impact of economic and regulatory structures, but also through the pressures drawing both the Americans and the Europeans into areas of political uncertainty and friction. It forms the basis for mutual involvement in institutional structures, and for an evolving division of labour in dealing with matters of mutual concern. It is also hard work, demanding of its practitioners constant attention and adjustment, and carrying the inevitable risk of uncertainty, misunderstanding and confusion. The evidence from this study is that this is what is happening in the current evolution of US/EC relations.

It is just such competitive cooperation which has operational relevance and significance, rather than any 'grand designs' or aspirational rhetoric aiming at a revised special relationship between the US and the EC. What is needed is to focus on how to strengthen cooperation rather than pursuing will o' the wisps. Even then, the complexity of linkages means that a way must be found to set up some kind of automatic mechanisms for the treatment of important but more mundane matters, such as trade and investment issues, in order to allow more time and energy for cooperation in areas in which there are perceived to be mutual interests. In other words, a framework must be created that allows competition to take place but also contains it. Steps must also be taken to strengthen the processes for dealing with cooperation in monetary and foreign or security policy.

What is to be done?

Given that the existing state of US/EC relations conforms to a model of competitive cooperation and uneven but intense mutual engagement, the question for policy is what needs to be done – or what can be done – to accentuate the positive and minimize the negative aspects of the situation. Nor can one forget that the circumstances are of economic and policy interdependence, in which domestic preoccupations vie with, and intersect with, the insistent demands of international order. There is an accumulated body of political and social learning, which contains positive and negative lessons. There is a plethora of institutions with more or less well-defined remits and roles, and with varying degrees of recognition and legitimacy. There are interests capable of expression at many levels, with the consequent problems of aggregation and calculation of costs and benefits. We have ruled out 'grand designs' and a comprehensive settlement of the 'aspirational approach'. What is to be done?

Conclusions

The complex nature of the linkages described in this volume suggest that both the US and the EC face formidable problems in developing coherent and comprehensive approaches to policy coordination. In the past there was a largely positive effort to insulate security cooperation from economic or trade competition. But the end of the cold war threatens to sweep away the unwritten agreement that one does not rock the boat of common security by scrapping over trade issues. Without the security blanket to dampen economic competition the respective authorities will have to cover the linkages between the various policy areas and ensure that they can deliver the support of the domestic constituencies for the package of agreements reached. As the preceding chapters suggest, neither the EC nor the US are proving very successful in achieving such an ambitious objective. In the case of the US, it is currently primarily a question of delivering the domestic constituencies. In the case of the EC, there is a major problem defining a coherent external policy. Although the provisions of Maastricht for a common foreign and security policy could mark a significant step forward, the popular censure of the distance of some EC policymaking from the electorate, which is now intensifying, shows the EC is also having (though somewhat different) problems delivering its domestic constituencies. In short, it is unrealistic to expect either the EC or the US to be able to achieve the kind of coherence and consistency of policy which would enable negotiators to sit down together and agree on policy coordination. The future relationship between the US and the EC will be more pluralistic, with interaction continuing in trade, economic policy and foreign and security policy fields.

One important advance would be to seek to ease the burden on the relationship that is imposed by detailed trade and investment issues. This is not a new proposal. In 1989, for example, the European Parliament and Congress jointly argued for a bilateral dispute settlement procedure to deal with relatively minor trade disputes which, because of the precedents involved, can swallow up a disproportionate amount of time and energy on the part of skilled US and EC negotiators. What is advocated here is a broader, more far-reaching approach which would strengthen the processes for dealing with such issues. If successful, it would have the further advantage of providing a sounder common economic base for transatlantic cooperation in other areas.

Trade and investment relations are unstable because market-led interpenetration and interdependence across the Atlantic has not been matched by policy initiatives. Broadly speaking, one can envisage three scenarios for EC/US commercial relations: a move to help policy keep pace with market integration; retaining the policy status quo; or disintegration with negative regional bloc- building. More policy integration is problematic because of continued systemic differences; the status quo, however, is unstable (for reasons already noted) and could easily slip into disintegration. Ideally, the successful EC process of integration should be extended to the transatlantic area, meaning that there should be an agreement on mutual recognition within a multilateral framework: i.e. the 'minimum essential requirements' would be as set out in GATT agreements. This would promote policy integration between the US and the EC without undermining multilateralism. But the US Congress, for one, is not ready to cede this degree of sovereignty. US policy responses to interdependence have tended to take the form of initiatives towards reaching agreed (i.e. harmonized) multilateral rules and, when this has failed, a reversion to unilateral definitions of what the US believes *ought* to be the multilateral rules. There has also been a growing preoccupation with results.

As formal mutual recognition is unlikely to be politically acceptable, the most fruitful approach is therefore to develop a form of *competition among rules*. In practice the high level of interdependence is already bringing this about and thus contributing to an approximation of policies. The EC and the US should aim to promote such forces by explicitly accepting that neither can expect its rules to prevail in bilateral or multilateral negotiations. In other words, there would be a *de facto* mutual recognition. As in the EC, this would call for agreement on minimum essential requirements, which would in turn have to be agreed in the GATT, BIS or other multilateral bodies. There would also have to be an effective dispute settlement, which could be based on strengthened GATT procedures agreed during the Uruguay Round of negotiations. If progress can be made in this area, some of the burden of detailed technical negotiations on trade and market access issues could be lifted from US and EC negotiators.

The second area in which there is a need for greater cooperation is that of general economic coordination, particularly monetary and exchange-rate policies. The turbulence in exchange rates during 1992, and the realignment of September 1992, have been a significant setback for the EC. In so far as the EC, or a core of its member states, plays a growing role in monetary and exchange-rate policies, it would be in the interests of EC/US relations, but also in the US interest, to develop *channels of cooperation between the European and US authorities on monetary policy*, rather than wait until the EC is in a position to neglect the external implications of its policy. The administration's benign neglect of the dollar in the early 1990s may prove to be the last time the US is able to afford such a posture.

There seems little doubt that such cooperation will be needed. Whatever the differences between EC and US interests and the increased preoccupations of both with domestic affairs, there will still be bilateral and global issues on which there is a strong case for working together. Joint management of a new world order may be impracticable and possibly undesirable, given the benefit of maintaining genuine multilateral structures. But unless the EC and the US can agree on a common agenda and cooperate in supporting the international economic and political orders, a dangerous vacuum will develop.

This should be done by *continuing to strengthen political cooperation* through, for example, existing US links with European Political Cooperation and EPC links with US policy formulation. These links are not yet consistently good and fluctuate depending on which country has the presidency of the EC. There is also a need for a genuine two-way process, which could be facilitated by using the institution-rich environment more effectively. At many points in this study, the 'crowding' or overlapping of institutions in specific issue areas has been noted. Whereas this is long established and manageable in the economic domain (despite continuing problems surrounding the status of the Community), the demands of political and security questions have exposed new strains and limitations. Chapter 4 has touched on many of these; it has also revealed the ways in which clusters of institutions, and of institutional 'occasions', can provide a useful basis for coordination of strategy and the building of coalitions. Thus, in June and July 1992, the coincidence of key meetings for NATO, WEU, the CSCE, the Community and the G7 provided a density of contacts and a range of institutional contexts within which the problems of politics and security could be approached from a variety of angles. The use and exploitation of such occasions may not be a perfect solution to the problems of transatlantic policy coordination, and it raises the subsequent question of how coalitions can be translated into action on the ground, as in the case of Yugoslavia. None the less, there are signs that this form of cooperation is becoming a feature of the diplomatic landscape, shaping the expectations of policymakers.

Willy Brandt once memorably contended that the greatest problem facing the then West Germany in international life was the need for Germans to 'recognize themselves'. The same might be said of the new transatlantic relations of the 1990s: the need is for self-recognition on the part of those most heavily engaged in them. The history of European/ American relations demonstrates that grand declarations are a necessary part of their evolution, but that their substance is to be found in the laying of sound economic foundations, day-to-day processes of policy interaction, and the building of institutional and elite networks around broad issue areas. This truth should not be ignored in the transformed conditions of the 1990s, whatever the pressures. There is a call, on the one hand, for a formal treaty relationship between the two sides of the Atlantic and, on the other, for some form of divorce. The Transatlantic Declaration has given the process its formal foundation and should prepare the way for further work. But it will be important for policy-makers to translate the process of coordination and network-building into action. If they do not, the result will be uncertainty, and may be disaster. If they do – and there are signs that they may be doing so almost without recognizing it – the United States and the European Community can function as the focal points of a more robust world order.

NOTES

Chapter 1: The challenges of a transformed world

1 The text of the Berlin address and the later speech on the same subject by James Baker to the Aspen Institute in Berlin during June 1991 can be found in *Berlin Speeches* (London: Embassy of the USA, US Information Service, July 1991). The Transatlantic Declaration, or *Declaration on EC-US Relations*, can be found in *Europe/Documents*, no. 1622, Brussels, 23 November 1990.

2 See M. Smith, '"The Devil You Know": The United States and A Changing European Community', *International Affairs*, vol. 68, no. 1, January 1992, pp. 103–20.

3 See, for example, B. Buzan *et al.*, *The European Security Order Recast: Scenarios for the Post-Cold War Era* (London: Pinter, 1990); A. Hyde-Price, *European Security Beyond the Cold War: Four Scenarios for the Year 2010* (London: Sage for the Royal Institute of International Affairs, 1991); F. Heisbourg, ed., *The Strategic Implications of Change in the Soviet Union* (London: Macmillan for the International Institute for Strategic Studies, 1990); R. Ullman, *Securing Europe* (Princeton, NJ: Princeton U.P., 1991).

4 See, for example. J. Schott, 'Trading Blocs and the World Trading System', *The World Economy*, vol. 14, no. 1, 1991, pp. 1–19; and R.C. Hine, ed., 'Regionalism and the Integration of the World Economy', *Journal of Common Market Studies*, vol. XXX, no. 2, June 1992.

5 Robert Mauthner and Lionel Barber, 'Bush calls on Europe to clarify role in NATO', *Financial Times*, 8 November 1991, p. 1.

6 Smith, 'The Devil You Know', pp. 105–9. See also D. Calleo, *Beyond American Hegemony: The Future of the Western Alliance* (New York: Basic Books, 1987), esp. Part II.

7 See Michael T. Clark and Simon Serfaty, eds., *New Thinking and Old*

112

Realities (Washington, DC: Seven Locks Press, 1991); Buzan *et al.*, *The European Security Order Recast.*

8 See, for example, I.M. Destler *et al.*, *Our Own Worst Enemy: The Unmaking of American Foreign Policy* (New York: Simon and Schuster, 1984); R. Rose, *The Postmodern President: The White House Meets the World* (Chatham, NJ: Chatham House Publishers, 1988).

9 For reasons of space and focus, this study excludes any detailed consideration of the EC/US/Japan 'triangle'. Readers are referred to the growing range of studies in this area, for example: L. Thurow, *Head to Head: The Coming Economic Battle Among Japan, Europe, and America* (New York: William Morrow, 1992); J. Bergner, *The New Superpowers: Germany, Japan, the US, and the New World Order* (New York: St. Martin's Press, 1991).

10 See Calleo, *Beyond American Hegemony*; also M. Smith, *Western Europe and the United States: The Uncertain Alliance* (London: George Allen and Unwin, 1984), esp. Chapter 5.

Chapter 2: Domestic preoccupations and international identities

1 The extensive 'declinist' literature is centred on: P. Kennedy, *The Rise and Fall of the Great Powers* (London: Unwin Hyman, 1988); J. Nye, jr, *Bound to Lead: The Changing Nature of American Power* (New York: Basic Books, 1990); and H. Nau, *The Myth of America's Decline* (New York: Oxford University Press, 1990). See also D. Calleo, *Beyond American Hegemony: The Future of the Western Alliance* (New York: Basic Books, 1987), and R.W. Tucker and D. Hendrickson, *The Imperial Temptation: The New World Order and America's Purpose* (New York: Council on Foreign Relations, 1992.

2 See R. Reich, *The Work of Nations: Preparing Ourselves for 21st Century Capitalism* (New York: Knopf, 1991); R. Hormats, 'The Roots of American Power', *Foreign Affairs*, vol. 70, no. 3, Summer 1991, pp. 132–49.

3 A. Friedberg, 'The Changing Relationship between Economics and National Security', *Political Science Quarterly*, vol. 106, no. 2, Summer 1991, pp. 265–76; 'Searching for Security in a Global Economy', *Daedalus*, vol. 120, no. 4, Fall 1991. *The Economist* captured part of the feeling in an article published on 18 January 1992 (pp. 11–12): 'Sam, Sam the Paranoid Man'.

4 Hormats, 'The Roots of American Power'. See also Norman J. Ornstein, 'Foreign Policy and the 1992 Election', *Foreign Affairs*, vol. 71, no. 3, Summer 1992; J.K. Galbraith, *The Culture of Contentment* (London: Sinclair Stevenson, 1992).

5 N. Ornstein, 'Foreign Policy and the 1992 Election'. See also L. Thurow, *Head to Head: The Coming Economic Battle Among Japan, Europe and*

America (New York: William Morrow, 1992); R. Vernon and D. Spar, *Beyond Globalism: Remaking American Foreign Economic Policy* (New York: Free Press, 1989).

6 See R. Rose, *The Postmodern President: The White House Meets The World* (Chatham, N.J.: Chatham House Publishers, 1988); M. Pugh and P. Williams, eds., *Superpower Politics: Change in the United States and the Soviet Union* (Manchester: Manchester University Press, 1990), esp. Chapters 3–6.

7 W. Pfaff, 'Redefining World Power', *Foreign Affairs*, vol. 70, no. 1, 1991, pp. 34–48; M. Mandelbaum, 'The Bush Foreign Policy', *Foreign Affairs*, vol. 70, no. 1, 1991, pp. 5–22. Different responses to the changing situation are outlined in J. Martin, 'New Scripts for Bush and Clinton', *Financial Times*, 10 August 1992, p. 12.

8 See Mandelbaum, 'The Bush Foreign Policy'; T. Diebel, 'Bush's Foreign Policy: Mastery and Inaction', *Foreign Policy*, no. 84, Fall 1991, pp. 3–23.

9 Ornstein, 'Foreign Policy and the 1992 Election'; Martin, 'New Scripts for Bush and Clinton'; Michael Prowse, 'Mr Bush and the Churchill Syndrome', *Financial Times*, 30 December 1991; 'Greeting America's Salesman', *The Economist*, 4 January 1992, pp. 43–4.

10 Diebel, 'Bush's Foreign Policy'. It was widely noted during the Democratic Party convention of July 1992 that Bill Clinton devoted only 141 words of his acceptance address to foreign policy issues.

11 For the flavour of debates about the role of the EC in the 'new Europe', see W. Wallace, *The Transformation of Western Europe* (London: Pinter for the Royal Institue of International Affairs, 1990); G. Treverton, ed., *The Shape of the New Europe* (New York: Council on Foreign Relations, 1991).

12 See W. Sandholtz and J. Zysman, '1992: Recasting the European Bargain', *World Politics*, vol. 42, no. 1, October 1989, pp. 95–128; S. Hoffmann, 'The European Community and 1992', *Foreign Affairs*, vol. 68 , no. 4, Fall 1989, pp. 27–47. For broader treatments, see J. Pinder, *European Community: The Making of a Union* (London: Oxford University Press, 1991); W. Wallace, ed., *The Dynamics of European Integration* (London: Pinter for the Royal Institute of International Affairs, 1990); A. Sbragia, ed., *Europolitics: Institutions and Policymaking in the "New" European Community* (Washington, DC: Brookings Institution, 1992).

13 See H. Wallace, 'The Europe that Came in From the Cold', *International Affairs*, vol. 67, no. 4, October 1991, pp. 647–64; D. Allen and M. Smith, 'The European Community in the New Europe: Bearing the Burden of Change', *International Journal*, vol. 47, no. 1, Winter 1991–2, pp. 1–28. The broader context is covered in W. Wallace, *The Transformation of Western Europe*, and in H. Wallace, ed., *The Wider Western Europe: Reshaping the EC/EFTA Relationship* (London: Pinter for the Royal Institute of International Affairs, 1991).

14 See W. Wallace, *The Transformation of Western Europe*; Treverton, *The Shape of the New Europe*; Allen and Smith, 'The European Community in the New Europe'. See also J. Pinder, *The European Community and Eastern Europe* (London: Pinter for the Royal Institute of International Affairs, 1991); R. Rummel, ed., *Toward Political Union: Planning a Common Foreign and Security Policy in the European Community* (Boulder, Col.: Westview Press, 1992).

15 The mood was well captured by two supplements published in July 1992: 'Into the Void', *The Economist*, 11 July 1992; 'Europe: State of the Union', *Financial Times*, 1 July 1992.

16 W. Wallace, *The Transformation of Western Europe*; Allen and Smith, 'The European Community in the New Europe'.

17 'The Other Fortress Europe', *The Economist*, 1 June 1991, pp. 47–8; 'Strangers Inside the Gates', *The Economist*, 15 February 1992, pp. 17–20; J. Eyal, 'Refugee Crisis the Bitter Harvest of Europe's Inaction', *The Guardian*, 29 July 1992, p. 6.

18 'Into the Void', *The Economist*, 11 July 1992, notes the challenge to the established state/Community nexus. For discussion of the broader issue, see A. Sbragia, *Europolitics*, esp. Chapter 8; G. Treverton, *The Shape of The New Europe*, esp. Chapter 3; and R. Keohane and S. Hoffmann, eds., *The New European Community: Decision-making and Institutional Change* (Boulder, Col.: Westview Press, 1991), esp. Chapter 1.

19 H. Wallace, 'The Europe that Came in From the Cold'.

20 For an 'official' interpretation of the prospects for the New World Order, see S. Sloan, 'The US Role in a New World Order: Prospects for George Bush's Global Vision', Congressional Research Service Report 91-294 RCO, 28 March 1991. See also R. Tucker and D. Hendrickson, 'The Imperial Temptation: The New World Order and America's Purpose', *The Fletcher Forum of World Affairs*, Special Issue, 'What's New About the New World Order?' vol. 15, no. 2, Summer 1991. The notion of the 'lonely superpower' was coined by Charles Krauthammer: C. Krauthammer, 'The Lonely Superpower', *New Republic*, 29 July 1991, pp. 23–7. Uncertainties and debate in the economic and industrial sphere are captured in Clyde Prestowitz, jr, 'Beyond Laissez-faire', *Foreign Policy*, Summer 1992, pp. 67–87; Prestowitz is a longtime advocate of an interventionist trade and industrial policy.

21 See Treverton, *The Shape of the New Europe*, esp. Chapter 7; Allen and Smith, 'The European Community in the New Europe'. For a view on the ways in which the EC and Japan had become factors in the 1992 Presidential election, see M. Walker, 'Feeble Allies Dash Bush's High Hopes', *The Guardian*, 2 July 1992, p. 12.

Chapter 3: Changing roles in the world economy

1 See CSIS report, *Beyond 1992* (Washington, DC: Center for Strategic and International Studies).

2 See Arlene E. Wilson, 'Economic and Monetary Union' in *Europe and the United States: Competition and Cooperation in the 1990s* (Washington, DC: Congressional Research Service, 1992), for a summary of the motivation and progress of the negotiations on EMU.

3 In July 1992 there were conflicting estimates of the scale of this deflationary effect. A widely reported IMF study suggested that there would be a 0.75% reduction in EC GDP, concentrated in the countries which had to take the toughest action. This report also suggested that the growth gains, from reduced transaction costs, etc., would compensate for short-term losses in the medium term.

4 Michael Smith and David Allen, 'The European Community in the New Europe: Bearing the Burden of Change', *International Journal*, vol. 47, no. 1, Winter 1991–2.

5 See Articles 130 (a–e), on economic and social cohesion, of the Treaty of European Union; the Protocol on Social Policy and the Agreement on Social Policy concluded by the member states, with the exception of the UK; and the provisions on social dialogue in Articles 3 and 4 of the Agreement. Treaty on European Union, Luxembourg, 1992.

6 For example, the latest European Commission report on national subsidy programmes finds a total of 36bn ECU was spent on average every year in the EC between 1988 and 1990 to support European manufacturing, or an average of 3.5% of EC value added (down from 4% of value added in 1986-8). See 'Third Report on State Aids in the European Community', Commission of the EC, July 1992.

7 For a summary of EC industrial policy proposals, see *Official Journal of the European Communities*, C 178, 15 July 1992.

8 For a balanced treatment of this issue see *Competing Economies: America, Europe and the Pacific Rim* (Washington, DC: Office of Technology Assessment, 1991).

9 See Stephen Woolcock, *Market Access Issues in EC-US Relations: Trading Partners or Trading Blows?* (London: Pinter for the Royal Institute of International Affairs, 1991) for a more detailed discussion of this point.

10 For a brief summary of these differences, see *Economic Insights*, Institute of International Economics, Washington, DC, Spring 1992.

11 See Michel Albert, *Capitalisme contre capitalisme* (Paris: Seuil, 1992), for a treatment of these differences.

12 See Woolcock, *Market Access Issues*, for further discussion of this point.

13 In some cases the Commission has exercised discretionary power such as in the implementation of anti-dumping procedures.

14 It is possible to argue that they do not because each has tried to limit the extension of tight GATT discipline over national trade remedies, such as anti-dumping actions or the type of measures covered by Section 301. It would, of course, be easy to sign up to GATT agreements and then disregard them. The fact that neither the EC nor the US do this reflects a desire to avoid undermining what already exists.

15 Franco-German relations were politically sensitive because Germany was not prepared to leave France isolated in its opposition to compromise on agriculture at a time when Franco-German relations were already strained over the issue of German unification. Against the high politics of unification and the future shape of Europe, even the GATT assumed a low priority during 1990 and much of 1991.

16 See Woolcock, 'Europe and Trade Diplomacy', in Jonathan Story (ed.), *The New Europe*, forthcoming.

17 In this sense it is correct to see EMU as a defensive reaction. See Smith and Allen, 'The European Community in the New Europe'.

18 On the other hand, the varying effects of external shocks on individual countries could force them to adopt differing fiscal policies and thus could add to the difficulties of maintaining fiscal discipline.

19 In a speech in Annapolis in September 1990, Robert Zellick, then adviser for international economic affairs to Secretary of State Baker, and later Under-Secretary of State for Economic Affairs, spoke of three scenarios for the EC: as an international actor, as an itinerant player and as a large Switzerland. The description of the EC as a large Switzerland, with its implication of stability, is not entirely apt. A more appropriate analogy might be to the US during the period of benign neglect of the dollar.

20 There were, however, a number of congressional hearings on the subject after Maastricht had been agreed.

21 Stephen D. Cohen, *The Making of United States International Economic Policy* (New York: Praeger, 1981), 2nd edition.

22 See text of speech at Boston University, *Financial Times*, 22 May 1989. The linkages between US/Community and US/member state relations are illustrated by the fact that the speech was given in front of President Mitterrand, who was visiting Bush at the time.

23 'A New Europe and a New Atlanticism', Berlin Press Club, 12 December 1989.

24 See *Financial Times*, 28 February 1990.

25 See *Le Monde*, 22 November 1990.

26 See Alfred Kingon, 'Good News, Bad News About 1992', *The International Economy,* July/August 1988.

27 It has been suggested that the best way forward for the US in international policymaking, given its relative loss of power, would be through forming such coalitions. See Joseph Nye, 'Soft Power' in *Foreign Policy*, Fall 1990.

Chapter 4: The changing political order

1 The general issue of European and international order, and its relationship to Euro-Atlantic relations, is covered in G. Treverton, ed., *The Shape of the New Europe* (New York: Council on Foreign Relations, 1992), especially Stanley Hoffmann, 'Balance, Concert, Anarchy, or None of the Above', pp. 194–220. See also D. Allen and M. Smith, 'The European Community in the New Europe; Bearing the Burden of Change', *International Journal*, vol. 47, no. 1, Winter 1991–2, pp. 1–28, and R.W. Tucker and D.C. Hendrickson, *The Imperial Temptation: The New World Order and America's Purpose* (New York: Council on Foreign Relations, 1992), esp. Part One.

2 See J. Pinder, *The European Community and Eastern Europe* (London: Pinter for the Royal Institute of International Affairs, 1991).

3 See Pinder, *The European Community and Eastern Europe*; I. Lederer, ed., *Western Approaches to Eastern Europe* (New York: Council on Foreign Relations, 1992).

4 The effects were perhaps most noticeable in the Bush administration's policies. See T. Diebel, 'Bush's Foreign Policy: Mastery and Inaction', *Foreign Policy*, no. 84, Fall 1991, pp. 3–23; and M. Mandelbaum, 'The Bush Foreign Policy', *Foreign Affairs*, vol. 70, no. 1, 1991, pp. 5–22.

5 See M. Walker, 'Blinkered Bush Blows the Chance of a Lifetime', *The Guardian*, 16 January 1991, p. 10; M. Walker, `Bush Weighs Case for Baltic Sanctions', *The Guardian*, 23 January 1991, p. 11.

6 See L. Freedman, 'Order and Disorder in the New World', *Foreign Affairs*, vol. 71, no. 1, 1992, pp. 20–37; M. Mandelbaum, 'Coup de Grace: The End of the Soviet Union, *Foreign Affairs*, vol. 71, no. 1, 1992, pp. 164–83.

7 The text of Baker's Princeton speech on 'America and the Collapse of the Soviet Empire: What has to be done' can be found in `US Initiating World Conference to help Soviets', *Official Text* (London: US Information Service) 13 December 1991. For comment on the conference itself, see A. Robinson and D. Buchan, 'Donors Meet to Coordinate Aid for CIS Republics', *Financial Times*, 22 January 1992, p. 2.

8 See 'Bolder Still and Bolder', *The Economist*, 5 October 1991, pp. 16–17, and 'A New Nuclear Order', *The Economist*, 5 October 1991, pp. 47–8, for details of the arms control effort and its implications for other European countries including EC members.

9 See Wolfram Hanrieder, 'Germany, the New Europe, and the Transatlantic Connection', *International Journal*, vol. 46, no. 3, Summer 1991, pp. 394–419.

10 The American position was set out by President Bush in a speech at Oklahoma State University on 4 May 1990; see 'Bush Says United Germany Should Belong to NATO', *Official Text* (London: US Information Service), 8 May 1990. See also A. Moens, 'American Diplomacy and

German Unification', *Survival*, vol. 33, no. 6, November/December 1991, pp. 531–45. For the more general issue of German/American partnership, see R. Asmus, 'Germany and America: Partners in Leadership?', *Survival*, vol. 33, no. 6, November/December 1991, pp. 546–66.

11 On the evolution of European Community foreign and security policy debate during 1991, see T. Taylor, 'What Sort of Security for Western Europe?',*The World Today*, August/September 1991, pp. 138–42; C. Hill, 'The European Community: Towards a Common Foreign and Security Policy? *The World Today*, November 1991, pp. 189–93. A review from the United States perspective can be found in C. Guicherd, *A European Defense Identity: Challenge and Opportunity for NATO*, CRS Report for Congress 91-478 RCO (Washington, DC: Congressional Research Service, June 1991).

12 See Asmus, 'Germany and America: Partners in Leadership'; K. Kaiser, 'Germany's Unification', *Foreign Affairs*, vol. 70, no. 1, 1991.

13 On the relationship between unification and the broader issues of European order, see T. Carpenter, 'The New World Disorder', *Foreign Policy*, no. 84, Fall 1991, pp. 24–39; on the issue of German financial assistance to the former USSR, see W.R. Smyser, `USSR-Germany: A Link Restored', *Foreign Policy*, no. 84, Fall 1991, pp. 125–40.

14 See 'So Much Power, So Little Purpose', *The Economist*, 18 January 1992; Q. Peel, 'Damned if it does – and if it doesn't', *Financial Times*, 18 January 1992

15 See Carpenter, 'The New World Disorder'.

16 See, for example, the debate in mid-1992 about the constitutional position in relation to the use of force and participation in UN operations; D. Gow, 'Germany Ready to Widen Military Role', *The Guardian*, 23 July 1992, p. 10. More dramatically, the resignation of Defence Minister Gerhard Stoltenberg as the result of a dispute over arms sales to Turkey revealed the underliyng tensions over defence and foreign policy as a whole. See Q. Peel, `Germany Shoots itself in the Foot', *Financial Times*, 1 April 1992, p. 2.

17 For a discussion of this issue, see Hoffmann, 'Balance, Concert, Anarchy, or None of the Above', in Treverton, *The Shape of the New Europe*. See also M. Smith, 'Beyond the Stable State? Foreign Policy Challenges and Opportunities in the New Europe', in S. Smith and W. Carlsnaes, eds., *Foreign Policy Analysis and the New Europe* (London: Sage, 1992). On the role that could be played by the EC, see R. Rosecrance, 'Regionalism and the Post-Cold War Era', *International Journal*, vol. 46, no. 3, Summer 1991, pp. 373–93.

18 See R. Mauthner, 'The EC is Found Wanting', *Financial Times*, 31 July 1991, p. 17; A. Savill, 'Policy Shift Before Independence Day', *The Independent*, 4 July 1991, p. 9.

19 See Mauthner, 'The EC is Found Wanting', *Financial Times*, 31 July 1991; the comment by Poos is cited in D. Gardner, 'EC Dashes into its own Backyard', *Financial Times*, 1 July 1991, p. 2.

20 See E. Mortimer, 'Bosnia's Tragic Example', *Financial Times*, 27 May 1992, p. 19.

21 See S. Sullivan *et al.*, 'Europe the Feeble', *Newsweek*, 11 February 1991, pp. 26–8.

22 For an example of the expectations and issues, see G. Jeszensky, 'Nothing Quiet on the Eastern Front', *NATO Review*, June 1992, pp. 7–13. CSCE action over Nagorno-Kharabakh provided a concrete focus for many of the uncertainties: see R. Mauthner, 'Moves on Kharabakh War', *Financial Times*, 25 May 1992, p. 2. The later NATO Declaration on the Nagorno-Kharabakh situation can be found in *NATO Review*, June 1992, p. 10.

23 See A. Fenton Cooper, R. Higgott and K.R. Nossal, 'Bound to follow? Leadership and Followership in the Gulf Conflict', *Political Science Quarterly*, vol. 106, no. 3, Fall 1991, pp. 391–410; M. Brenner, 'The Alliance: A Gulf Post-Mortem', *International Affairs*, vol. 67, no. 4, 1991, pp. 665–78.

24 See J. Steele, 'Tinderbox in the Caucasus', *The Guardian*, 27 May 1992.

25 On the general issue of population movements, see F. Heisbourg, 'Population Movements in Post-Cold War Europe', *Survival*, vol. 33, no. 1, January/February 1991, pp. 31–44. Assessments of the 1992 refugee crisis can be found in: J. Dempsey, L. Silber and R Graham, 'Europe Fears Influx of Yugoslav Refugees', *Financial Times*, 19 May 1992, p. 2; 'An Inch Deeper into the Balkan Quagmire', *The Economist*, 18 July 1992, pp. 39–40.

26 On the general issue of non-proliferation, see J. Simpson and D. Howlett, 'Nuclear Non-Proliferation: the Way Forward', *Survival*, vol. 33, no. 6, November/December 1991, pp. 483–99. See also R. Mauthner, 'Force May be Needed to Stop Proliferation', *Financial Times*, 22 May 1992, p. 2; S. Tisdall, 'Baker to Offer Hi-Technology in Return for Curb on Arms Sales', *The Guardian*, 27 May 1992; F. Heisbourg, 'Arsenal in the Firing Line', *The Guardian*, 18 June 1992, on the position of the British and the French.

27 See the leader 'A Green Target for Mr Bush', *Financial Times*, 31 March 1992.

28 See, for example, 'Nuclear Alert: Can the West Move Fast Enough to Prevent Another Chernobyl?', *International Business Week*, 8 June 1992, pp. 16–21.

29 *London Declaration on a Transformed North Atlantic Alliance*, issued by the Heads of State and Government participating in the Meeting of the North Atlantic Council in London, 6 July 1990, *NATO Review*, August 1990, pp. 32–3.

30 See Colombo, 'European Security at a Time of Radical Change'. Others

were less confident, particularly about the extent to which the new 'institutional architecture' preserved a legitimate United States voice in European affairs. See, for example, T. Emerson *et al.*, 'Voice of America', *Newsweek*, 1 July 1991, pp. 10–11.

31 See E. Colombo, 'European Security at a Time of Radical Change', *NATO Review*, June 1992, pp. 3–7. The same issue also contains the text of the Oslo communiqué: *Communiqué of the Ministerial Meeting of the North Atlantic Council in Oslo, 4 June 1992, NATO Review*, June 1992, pp. 30–32. The issue of peacekeeping through the CSCE as raised at the Helsinki meeting is summarized in J. Dempsey, 'CSCE States to set up Peacekeeping forces', *Financial Times*, 9 July 1992, p. 3.

32 See R. Mauthner, 'New World Watchdog in Search of Bark and Bite', *Financial Times*, 24 March 1992.

33 See 'Watch this Space', *The Economist*, 18 July 1992, p. 41.

34 See E. Mortimer, 'Europe's security surplus', *Financial Times*, 4 March 1992, p. 12.